Especially for

....

From

....

Date

....

3-Minute Devotions

for

Mommy & Me

Encouraging Readings
for Parents & Kids

Stacey Thureen

BARBOUR BOOKS
An Imprint of Barbour Publishing, Inc.

© 2019 by Barbour Publishing, Inc.

ISBN 978-1-68322-948-3

Scripture quotations are taken from the New Life Version (NLV), copyright © 1969 and 2003 by Barbour Publishing, Inc. All rights reserved.

Cover and Interior Illustrations: Eva Morales

Published by Barbour Books, an imprint of Barbour Publishing, Inc., 1810 Barbour Drive, Uhrichsville, Ohio 44683, www.barbourbooks.com

Our mission is to inspire the world with the life-changing message of the Bible.

Member of the
Evangelical Christian
Publishers Association

Printed in China.

06383   0419   DS

Dedication

To my children

3-Minute Devotions for Mommy and Me is a devotional for you and your little one(s), ages 3 to 7. Featuring colorful illustrations, this book is a fun way to encourage and develop the important habit of learning about God and His Word. These kid-friendly devotions offer a few short minutes to spend time together, explore simple truths found in the Bible, and relate them to everyday life in a way that young children can understand. Each of the entries is broken down into three sections (Talk about it, Read about it, Pray about it), and is written in your own point of view as you engage with your child(ren).

Our Forever Friend

"I do not call you servants that I own anymore.
A servant does not know what his owner is doing.
I call you friends, because I have told you everything
I have heard from My Father."

John 15:15

TALK ABOUT IT

What makes a good friend?

READ ABOUT IT

Friends are fun, helpful, loving, and kind. We can go to them when we want to play or when we need support and encouragement. But sometimes they make mistakes. They might forget to keep a secret or decide they do not want to play with you. Jesus is our Best Friend forever though. No matter what happens in our relationships, Jesus will always love us and be there for us! That is something we can continually count on.

PRAY ABOUT IT

Dear God, we're so thankful that You are our Best Friend. Even though we all make mistakes and let other people down sometimes, You will never do that to us. Thank You for that! Amen.

God Creates

*In the beginning God made from
nothing the heavens and the earth.*

GENESIS 1:1

TALK ABOUT IT

What things do you like to make and why do you like making
them?

READ ABOUT IT

If the items you like to make are arts and craft projects, for
example, each of the pieces you use were made and specifically
designed for a purpose. And did you know that where those items
were made, someone had to make the necessary tools in order to
create them? Even though there were so many people involved
in designing these things, God is the One who ultimately creates
everything and everyone! God is so big that He even created the
heavens and the earth!

PRAY ABOUT IT

Dear God, from the pictures we create, to the crafts we make,
to the blocks we use to build with, we are thankful for Your creativity! You used the hands, feet, and minds of people to help
make what we use. Amen.

God Loves Us

*I pray that you will be able to understand
how wide and how long and how high
and how deep His love is.*

EPHESIANS 3:18

TALK ABOUT IT

What is the biggest thing you can think of?

READ ABOUT IT

Think of the tallest building, roller coaster, or the biggest mountain that you've ever seen. Something so tall that you can't even see the top! Think of the deepest water. So deep that no matter how hard you try to touch the bottom, you could never hold your breath long enough. I love you more than the tallest, widest, longest, deepest thing you can imagine! But God's love is bigger than my love for you, little one. God has known you and me since before we were born, and His love for us will last forever—for *eternity*!

PRAY ABOUT IT

Dear God, Your love for us is higher than the sky and deeper than the ocean. It makes us feel special that You love us so much. We love You too. Amen.

God Heals

*He heals those who have a broken
heart. He heals their sorrows.*

PSALM 147:3

TALK ABOUT IT

Recall a time when you were sad after what someone said or
did to you. What was that experience like? Since then, how have
you gotten better?

READ ABOUT IT

Being hurt by someone or experiencing pain from an incident
isn't fun. As your mommy, I feel sad to see you in tears because
I care about you. I want to help you feel better. As a child of
God, when you are down He cares for you. I love you and He
loves you even more than we can imagine! The Bible says that
Jesus knows your pain. It might take some time, but God will
help you get well.

PRAY ABOUT IT

Dear God, You are our greatest Healer. Thank You for taking our
tears and using them for good. Amen.

God Keeps Us Safe

I will lie down and sleep in peace.
O Lord, You alone keep me safe.

PSALM 4:8

TALK ABOUT IT

When you feel scared or alone, what helps you feel safe? Is it a stuffed animal or singing a certain song?

READ ABOUT IT

Whether it's a thunderstorm or being away from an adult for a few minutes, there are things in life that can feel very scary. There are experiences in my life that have caused me to feel alone or afraid too. God promises to be with us though. This verse speaks clearly to our need for comfort and security. I'm here for you, little one, whenever you need me. But you know what? Even when I can't be there for you immediately, God is already right there watching over you.

PRAY ABOUT IT

Dear God, thank You for protecting us and for keeping us safe. Thank You for watching over us all of the time and for giving us Your peace. Amen.

We Can Sing Songs to God

Praise the Lord! For it is good to sing praises to our God. For it is pleasing and praise is right.

<small>PSALM 147:1</small>

Talk about it

What are some creative ways that you like to show gratitude and thankfulness toward others?

Read about it

It makes my heart so happy when you express your joy for life and others through your words, your hands, and your feet. God also loves it when we express just how much we adore Him through our voices, hands, and feet. The Bible says that we can do so by singing songs to Him! So, let's get up and give it a try—together!

Pray about it

Dear God, thank You for blessing us with so many fun and creative ways to show our thanks to You and others. May we continue to sing songs of praise with our lips, in and through our actions. Amen.

God Knows You

*You look over my path and my lying down.
You know all my ways very well.*

PSALM 139:3

TALK ABOUT IT

What helps you feel like someone really knows you well?

READ ABOUT IT

A best friend knows a lot about you, right? They know what you like and don't like. They probably know some of your secrets too. As your mommy, I know a lot about you too. I know what you like to eat and drink. I know how to make things for you, just the way you like them. But God knows everything about you! In fact, He knows that you and I are reading this devotional together right now! Isn't that amazing? The Bible says He knows all of our ways.

PRAY ABOUT IT

Dear God, how can we not trust You? Thank You that You see all that we do. Thank You for watching over us. Amen.

God Provides for Us

And my God will give you everything you need
because of His great riches in Christ Jesus.

PHILIPPIANS 4:19

TALK ABOUT IT

Share with me about a time that you got exactly what you needed. Share with me about a time when you got exactly what you wanted.

READ ABOUT IT

God always provides for us. He will always meet our needs. The Bible talks about how you and I won't always get what we want. We will get what we need. In those moments when we get what we wish for, it doesn't happen very often, but sometimes it does. Whether we get what we need or what we long for, that is when we thank God for everything He has provided for us!

PRAY ABOUT IT

Dear Jesus, You are enough. You are all that we need. We're so thankful that everything we need has already been provided for us. All that we could ever desire is found in You! Amen.

God Knows Time

Dear friends, remember this one thing,
with the Lord one day is as 1,000 years,
and 1,000 years are as one day.

2 PETER 3:8

Talk about it

How many days make up one year? How many days do you think it takes to make up one thousand years?

Read about it

One thousand years can seem like a really, really long time! That's about 365,000 days! Amazingly, in God's timing, this is equal to one day! Can you believe it? One day! While God's ability to tell time is very different from ours, the bottom line is that sometimes things take a long while. The challenge is for us to be patient and trust His good and perfect plan while we wait.

Pray about it

Dear God, we are thankful that You know what time it is. Please help us to be patient when we wait for things like answers to prayer, birthday celebrations, or Christmastime. Amen.

God Helps Us

Our help is in the name of the Lord,
Who made heaven and earth.

PSALM 124:8

TALK ABOUT IT

Describe a time when you helped me or when I helped you.

READ ABOUT IT

I'm so grateful for the times you have been there to pitch in. And I appreciate it when you ask for my help too. We can also ask God to help us. When you and I forget to ask Jesus for help, the best part is that we often get to experience something wonderful. It's called grace. It's that moment we realize we didn't ask for help, but God provided it anyway through each other, someone else, or giving us an idea to help us figure things out.

PRAY ABOUT IT

Dear Father, it's pretty cool when we get to see You show up even when we forget to ask. Thank You for always being there ready to lead and guide us. Amen.

God Comforts Us

He gives us comfort in all our troubles. Then we can comfort other people who have the same troubles. We give the same kind of comfort God gives us.

2 CORINTHIANS 1:4

TALK ABOUT IT

What causes you to want to be comforted? A loud sound? Seeing something that looks scary?

READ ABOUT IT

A fire truck or ambulance siren, a scary cartoon character, hurtful words, even not doing well at something—all those things and more can leave us feeling scared. But God gives us a promise. When you and I are troubled, He will comfort us. Sometimes the comfort we receive is from each other: a hug, holding hands, or putting an arm around each other. Other times it might come in the form of encouraging words. Each one is a gift from God, given to us so that we can remember that He understands our feelings.

PRAY ABOUT IT

Dear God, we are grateful that when we feel down You are there to pick us up. Amen.

God's Spirit Is with Us

"But you will receive power when the Holy Spirit comes into your life. You will tell about Me in the city of Jerusalem and over all the countries of Judea and Samaria and to the ends of the earth."

ACTS 1:8

TALK ABOUT IT

What does it mean to have God's Spirit living inside of you?

READ ABOUT IT

Jesus told people that when He left they wouldn't be alone. He said the Holy Spirit would be with them and live within them. In fact, Jesus said that if He didn't leave there would be no reason for the Holy Spirit to come; it was more important for the Spirit to be here than for Him. Why? Because when we receive the Holy Spirit into our lives it gives us a unique and very important superpower. That is the ability to know right from wrong, good from bad.

PRAY ABOUT IT

Dear Jesus, thank You for giving us the Holy Spirit who helps us to live like You. Amen.

God Cares

Give all your worries to Him because He cares for you.

1 PETER 5:7

TALK ABOUT IT

When was the last time you felt worried about something? What was it that concerned you?

READ ABOUT IT

When you feel worried about something you can always come to me to talk about it. I might not know all of the right things to say or have the best answer. I will do my best to listen to you and pray for you though. But you know who cares for you more than I ever can? You know who knows all the answers before we even ask? God! So, in prayer, let's practice sharing our cares and concerns with our Creator, together.

PRAY ABOUT IT

Dear heavenly Daddy, we come to You with open hands. In these hands are the things that have been troubling us today. We ask that You take them from us and fill our hands with Your peace. Amen.

God Stands Up for Us

*"The Lord will fight for you.
All you have to do is keep still."*

Exodus 14:14

Talk about it

Describe a time when you felt angry and you wanted to fight back.

Read about it

Think back to a time you got really frustrated or mad. There are a lot of situations in life that can leave us feeling hurt. I love you so much, and unfortunately there are instances between you and me that can be challenging, leaving us feeling misunderstood. But God tells us what to do in those hard moments. We can just be still and pray to God for help. When we ask Him for wisdom, He will show us how to take care of the situation.

Pray about it

Dear God, when we feel upset, angry, hurt, offended, or mis-understood, help us to pray to You for help. Then, help us to be still and not act out until You show us what to do next. Amen.

God Knows When We Hurt

The Lord is near to those who have a broken heart.
And He saves those who are broken in spirit.

PSALM 34:18

TALK ABOUT IT

What do you think it means to have a broken heart?

READ ABOUT IT

Another way to describe a broken heart is to feel really, really sad or experience deep emotional hurt inside. At some point in life, we all might feel really down. We may want to cry or take a break from whatever we are doing. Did you know that in those moments we can talk to God about our situation? We sure can! We might not think or feel like He's close to us or that He cares, but He is right there with us and absolutely does care.

PRAY ABOUT IT

Dear heavenly Daddy, when we have a broken heart, thank You for being there with us. Thank You for comforting us and for seeing our tears. Amen.

Jesus Was a Carpenter

Is He not a Man Who makes things from wood?
Is He not the Son of Mary and the brother of James
and Joses and Judas and Simon? Do not His sisters
live here with us?" The people were ashamed
of Him and turned away from Him.

MARK 6:3

Talk about it

What would you like to be when you grow up?

Read about it

Before Jesus began His ministry work, He learned about wood-work. This skill taught Him about the art of using His hands. It required structure and technique. These disciplines learned early in life helped Jesus later in life. God has also placed skills in your life to continually develop. It is going to be so much fun to see how God will use them for good as you grow!

Pray about it

Dear God, please nurture the skills You've given us so that we can continue to grow and mature. May we use them for Your Kingdom work. Amen.

God Doesn't Like Sin

*If you know what is right to do but
you do not do it, you sin.*

JAMES 4:17

TALK ABOUT IT

What were the things you did today that may have caused someone to feel sad or disappointed?

READ ABOUT IT

To be honest, there are a lot of things that I do throughout the day that I know I shouldn't do but I do it anyway. When this happens, I might hurt or offend someone, especially God. Ultimately, this is called sin. Thankfully, we have a God who loves us and forgives us. So when you or I make a mistake we can go to God, tell Him what we did wrong, and ask for forgiveness. The Bible says that He is then faithful and just to forgive us of all of our wrongdoings.

PRAY ABOUT IT

Dear God, when I make a mistake and do what I know I ought not to do, please give me the ability to see it and ask for Your forgiveness. Amen.

God Forgives

If we tell Him our sins, He is faithful and we can depend on Him to forgive us of our sins. He will make our lives clean from all sin.

1 JOHN 1:9

TALK ABOUT IT

Tell me about a time you forgave someone for doing something wrong to you. What was that like? Did that person apologize?

READ ABOUT IT

We know that God doesn't like it when you and I sin. But He also knows that it will happen, so He is gracious with us. We get to experience God's forgiveness when we admit to Him what we've done. Like apologizing to a friend or saying you're sorry, we can do that with God. That is kind of what asking for forgiveness is all about. I think it's pretty awesome that we can go to God and be real with Him like this, don't you?

PRAY ABOUT IT

Dear God, we are amazed that when we confess our sins, You are faithful and just to forgive everything! Amen!

God Meets Our Needs

"Look at the birds. They do not plant seeds. They do not gather grain. They have no grain buildings for keeping grain. Yet God feeds them. Are you not worth more than the birds?"

LUKE 12:24

TALK ABOUT IT

What are some of the things that a mom needs to do to help her baby?

READ ABOUT IT

After you were born, there were a lot of things I needed to do in order to help keep you healthy and growing. I needed to feed you, change your diaper, clothe you, help you fall asleep, play with you, and hold you. As you have gotten older, your needs have changed but my role as your mommy is still the same. God also sees us and our needs. He takes care of and provides for all of us. Everything that I'm able to give you—food, a home, clothes—all comes from God.

PRAY ABOUT IT

Dear God, thank You for always meeting our needs. Amen.

Creation Reflects God's Image

Then God said, "Let Us make man like Us and let him be head over the fish of the sea, and over the birds of the air, and over the cattle, and over all the earth, and over every thing that moves on the ground."

GENESIS 1:26

TALK ABOUT IT

When you look in the mirror, what do you see?

READ ABOUT IT

When we look in the mirror we see a head with hair, eyes, ears, a nose, a mouth, a neck, arms, hands, belly, legs, and feet. The Bible says that we were made in the image of God. This means that God created us to not be Him, but we look similar to Him. He also created us to rule over a lot of things we see and interact with on earth. Pretty cool, huh?

PRAY ABOUT IT

Dear God, we don't know how You did it, but You created us! You created everything we see, feel, touch, and smell. Thank You! Amen.

We Can Trust God

Agree with Him in all your ways,
and He will make your paths straight.

PROVERBS 3:6

TALK ABOUT IT

What are some of the choices that you made today? Who helped you make those choices?

READ ABOUT IT

Reflect on all of the little and big choices that you made today. Maybe you had to ask for help from me, a teacher, or a friend when making those decisions. You know who else can help you with the choices that you make throughout the day? God! The Bible says that when we trust God, He will help us make good decisions. When we pray together, or when you pray on your own, let's ask God for help.

PRAY ABOUT IT

Dear God, thank You for being someone that we can rely on. When we're having a hard time making a choice, help us to ask You for help. Amen.

We Can Talk to God

*"Then you will call upon Me and come
and pray to Me, and I will listen to you."*
JEREMIAH 29:12

TALK ABOUT IT

What do you enjoy the most when you get to talk with someone
you know well?

READ ABOUT IT

Just like the way you and I can talk to a good friend, or each other,
God desires for us to talk to Him. In fact, He greatly encourages
an ongoing conversation with us. He wants to hear from you and
me on a regular basis. How do we do this? We just talk to Him.
He hears us and promises to listen. He also wants us to pray to
Him. So let's call on God together.

PRAY ABOUT IT

Dear Father, we are in awe of the fact that You can hear us right
now. Help us to continue to talk with You throughout our day.
Amen.

Jesus Is a Teacher

"You call Me Teacher and Lord. You are right because that is what I am."

JOHN 13:13

Talk about it

When you think about the teachers in your life, what makes them so special?

Read about it

The teachers that you and I have crossed paths with bring their own ideas, creativity, and talents to what they do. Whether it's at school, church, or an extracurricular activity, their knowledge, instruction, and experiences provide a foundation for learning and growth. Jesus was also called a teacher. Why? Because He helps guide and steer us in faith and in life. His understanding of God's Word inspires us to continue reading scripture and enjoy this quality time together.

Pray about it

Dear Father, we are so grateful for this time! Help us to remain in Your Word so that we may continue to learn from You, our greatest Teacher. We love You. Amen.

We Can Praise and Worship God

"The Lord is my strength and song. He is the One Who saves me. He is my God and I will praise Him. He is my father's God and I will honor Him."

EXODUS 15:2

TALK ABOUT IT

What are some words you have used to say good things about others? How about God?

READ ABOUT IT

When God created you and me, He gave us a mouth, teeth, tongue, and lips. We have a voice as well that can be used to sing songs. We can use our voice to praise others, including God. What is praise? It's an expression with our words, even our actions, that is positive. When we talk or sing about God in a good way, that brings praise to Him. Sharing good words about God with others also shows that we honor and love Him.

PRAY ABOUT IT

Dear heavenly Daddy, we love You! We invite You into our body and mind to help us speak good words about You to others. Amen.

God Speaks to Us

*"See! I stand at the door and knock. If anyone hears
My voice and opens the door, I will come in
to him and we will eat together."*

REVELATION 3:20

TALK ABOUT IT

What are some ways that you believe God speaks to you? To others?

READ ABOUT IT

God speaks to His children in many different ways. Sometimes He does it through nature and sometimes through other people. Sometimes we sense that we're supposed to do one thing instead of another. Most of all God talks to us through His Word, the Bible. The more you and I have this time together, reading God's Word and praying, the more we are following Him. This will help us to know right from wrong and understand Him better.

PRAY ABOUT IT

Dear God, we want to hear Your voice. Help us to continue to read these devotionals and read the Bible, so that we will know the difference between Your voice and another's. Amen.

God Hears Us

*We are sure that if we ask anything that
He wants us to have, He will hear us.*

1 JOHN 5:14

TALK ABOUT IT

When was the last time you talked about something important
to someone else, and you know they heard you? What was it
that you said to them?

READ ABOUT IT

It's great to know that we can talk about things that are important to us with others. It's really wonderful when we can share
those words with others and know they are listening to us. The
same is true with God. We can share what's on our mind with
Him. We can even ask Him for what we think we need or want,
and He promises to hear us. God promises that He's listening
to you because you're His child and He loves you!

PRAY ABOUT IT

Dear God, thank You for listening to us. Thank You that we can
ask You for anything and You will hear our words. Amen.

God Is Trustworthy

*Those who know Your name will put their trust
in You. For You, O Lord, have never left
alone those who look for You.*

PSALM 9:10

TALK ABOUT IT

Who are the people you trust? What is it about them that makes
them trustworthy?

READ ABOUT IT

When someone is trustworthy they often know us well, and we
feel comfortable around them. These people might be family
members or friends. These people love us, care about us, can
keep a secret, and cheer us on in life. God is someone we can
trust too. In fact, He wants us to trust Him more than anyone
else. Why? Because people are imperfect. We make mistakes,
we forget to keep a secret. But God doesn't make a mistake and
He will keep our secrets safe.

PRAY ABOUT IT

Dear God, thank You for never leaving us. Help us to trust You
when we forget to do so, or when we don't feel like it. Amen.

God Is Good

We know that God makes all things work together for the good of those who love Him and are chosen to be a part of His plan.

ROMANS 8:28

TALK ABOUT IT

Share about a time that you didn't make a good choice but there was a happy ending.

READ ABOUT IT

If we are honest, we all have made a wrong decision. Whether it's doing something we were told not to do, or not getting along with someone else. The list can go on and on. But you know what is so amazing? Even though we might not do what is right, God helps us make it right with Him. God promises that all things work together for good. This means that if you or I do something wrong, He will somehow help us and show us how to make it right!

PRAY ABOUT IT

Dear God, we know we're not perfect. We ask for Your help and guidance in all that we say and do. Amen.

God Is Gentle

*"Follow My teachings and learn from Me.
I am gentle and do not have pride.
You will have rest for your souls."*

MATTHEW 11:29

TALK ABOUT IT

What do you think it means to be gentle?

READ ABOUT IT

As your mommy, there have been times when I have told you to be careful with someone or something. Whether that's holding an item that could easily break or trying to give someone you know a hug. It is important that we are careful, because we do not always know our own strength. It's also important to be gentle because we don't want to hurt someone or something. Jesus is a great example of what it means to live this out. His teachings, the things we read about in the Bible, are at times kind, polite, and calm.

PRAY ABOUT IT

Dear Jesus, help us to be gentle. Help us to use good words. Help us to be thoughtful with our actions. Amen.

Jesus Is a Good Shepherd to Us

*"My sheep hear My voice
and I know them. They follow Me."*

JOHN 10:27

Talk about it

What is a shepherd?

Read about it

A shepherd is a person who tends to and guards their sheep. They are gentle and mindful of all of their flock. When one leaves the group, a shepherd goes out of their way to rescue that single sheep, making sure they are okay and reunited with the rest of the group. Jesus is often referred to as the Good Shepherd because He protects us, guides us, looks out for us, and watches over us. Like a shepherd, Jesus cares about you and me. It matters to Him that we get to have this time together.

Pray about it

Jesus, we love spending this time together. Thank You for tending to us so that we can have a relationship with you and with each other. What a blessing this is! Amen.

God Is Peace

The peace of God is much greater than the human mind can understand. This peace will keep your hearts and minds through Christ Jesus.

Philippians 4:7

Talk about it

What do you like to do during your quiet time?

Read about it

When there is a lot of noise in the car while I drive, I ask the family to be quiet or silent for a few minutes. Why? Because Mommy just wants it to be peaceful and safe. When there is quiet I can refocus so that our car ride conversations can be more fun. Jesus offers us an even greater peace. We can have things going on in our life that are loud and that take away quiet moments. But God's peace can help us to be still and not be moved by what's going on around us.

Pray about it

Dear God, equip us with the ability to be at peace with what is going on around us. Whatever we are walking through, may You be enough. Amen.

God Is Love

"For God so loved the world that He gave His only Son. Whoever puts his trust in God's Son will not be lost but will have life that lasts forever."

JOHN 3:16

TALK ABOUT IT

What does it mean to love somebody?

READ ABOUT IT

Love is a powerful word. It is also a powerful emotion. It is a way in which we express how much we care for one another. It can create a warm, fuzzy feeling on the inside of us. Love establishes a deep connection too. While there are many people in your life who adore you, including me, God loves you and me in a way that is hard to explain. What I do know is that it is downright beautiful and amazing!

PRAY ABOUT IT

Dear Father God, thank You for loving us in a way that is so amazing and awesome yet so hard to explain. We love You! Amen.

God Is with Us

*"Teach them to do all the things I have
told you. And I am with you always,
even to the end of the world."*

MATTHEW 28:20

TALK ABOUT IT

When have you felt like God was with you? When have you felt
like God was far away?

READ ABOUT IT

The Bible talks about the importance of doing what Jesus taught
us to do. Why? Probably because the more we live like Jesus is
living on the inside of us, the more it will feel like He is with
us. When you and I don't live with faith in our hearts, the more
distant we might feel from God. He is always with us, no matter
what! Let's pray to continue to live out what we know and have
learned about Jesus.

PRAY ABOUT IT

Dear God, we want to continue to learn about You and grow in
our faith. Help us to continue to do this, so that we will remain
close to You. Amen.

God Wants Us to Obey Our Parents

Children, as Christians, obey your parents.
This is the right thing to do.

Ephesians 6:1

Talk about it

What does it mean to obey God or even to obey Mommy and Daddy?

Read about it

Obedience is important. God wants us to listen to Him and do what He says, but He also wants children to listen to their parents' instructions and teachings. Why? Because when you are living with Daddy and me, you are living under our authority and leadership. Daddy and I are prayerfully seeking God for wisdom in how to best love and guide you. Daddy and I are held responsible before God to help meet your needs and to treat you the way He wants us to. This isn't easy because none of us are perfect. We can pray for God's help, though.

Pray about it

Dear God, help us to obey You. Help us to also be obedient to what You have commanded us to do as children and as parents. Amen.

Jesus Is like a Lamb

The next day John the Baptist saw Jesus coming to him. He said, "See! The Lamb of God Who takes away the sin of the world!"

JOHN 1:29

TALK ABOUT IT

When you see a little lamb, what do you like about them?

READ ABOUT IT

Jesus was often compared to being like a lamb because He resembled characteristics that were similar; His spirit was gentle, humble, and innocent. In His day, the sacrifice of a lamb was considered one way to have your sins taken away or forgiven. Because Jesus came into this world as a human being, to be the final sacrifice for our mistakes, He is also in this way like a lamb.

PRAY ABOUT IT

Dear Jesus, thank You for embracing us by forgiving us. Help us to embrace You as the Lamb of God. Amen.

God Wants Us to Love Our Neighbor

"You must love your neighbor as you love yourself."
MATTHEW 22:39

TALK ABOUT IT

What can you do to show that you love a neighbor as yourself?

READ ABOUT IT

This is one of God's greatest commandments, which is why Jesus made a point to teach about this when He lived on earth. To love a neighbor as yourself is another way of expressing the Golden Rule, which is to treat others the way that you want to be treated. Let's pray about ways that you and I can show love toward our neighbors. But it doesn't just have to be the people who live next door to us. Our neighbors are everyone we interact with on a regular basis too.

PRAY ABOUT IT

Dear God, help us to love each other the way that You want us to. Show us how we can care for and show Your love to others in our lives. Amen.

God Wants Us to Love Him

" 'You must love the Lord your God with all your heart
and with all your soul and with all your mind and
with all your strength.' This is the first Law."

MARK 12:30

TALK ABOUT IT

What are some things you have done to show God just how
much you love Him?

READ ABOUT IT

I love you and I know you love me. When we show our love for
each other, we do so with our actions and with our words. Besides
saying, "I love you," we also help each other, act patiently toward
each other, show kindness, and forgive one another. With God,
He wants us to love Him. He doesn't want us to put anyone or
anything else before Him. God wants to be first place in our lives.

PRAY ABOUT IT

Dear God, may You be first place in our heart, soul, and mind. Give
us the strength to love You the way You command us to. Amen.

Jesus Is King

For to us a Child will be born. To us a Son will be given. And the rule of the nations will be on His shoulders. His name will be called Wonderful, Teacher, Powerful God, Father Who Lives Forever, Prince of Peace.

ISAIAH 9:6

TALK ABOUT IT

How is a king supposed to act and treat his followers?

READ ABOUT IT

In this scripture verse we read a prediction about Jesus being king. Did you know that it was told *many* years before He was even born? In this text, we see that Jesus was meant to have a lot to do during His lifetime. He was to become the Prince of Peace, a king over the nations. Jesus was gracious, forgiving, humble, and kind. He was the opposite of how some kings act.

PRAY ABOUT IT

Dear King Jesus, thank You for ruling and reigning over our lives. We're so grateful that You came down from heaven in order to be the King of our faith! Amen.

God Wants Us to Tell the Truth

Lips that tell the truth will last forever,
but a lying tongue lasts only for a little while.

PROVERBS 12:19

TALK ABOUT IT

What does it mean when somebody tells a lie?

READ ABOUT IT

When we find out that someone has not told us the truth, it's no fun. Lies can hurt us and hurt others. Also, God doesn't like it when someone doesn't tell the truth. Dishonesty can cause you and me to lose our trust in a person. In the long run it can separate a close friend and ruin other relationships. In this verse from the book of Proverbs, we learn that lips that tell the truth will last forever. They do because when we tell the truth people want to talk to us, hear from us, and tell us things.

PRAY ABOUT IT

Dear God, may we aim to be honest even when it hurts. May we strive to tell the truth to help encourage another person we care about too. Amen.

God Wants Us to Be Thankful

Go into His gates giving thanks and into His holy place
with praise. Give thanks to Him. Honor His name.

PSALM 100:4

TALK ABOUT IT

What are some ways that our family has given thanks to God?

READ ABOUT IT

Thanksgiving is an awesome holiday. It's a day when we as a family come together to celebrate all of the good and wonderful things God has done in our lives. We get to eat a big meal, and some delicious desserts, while we listen to each other share stories of His goodness and faithfulness. But you and I don't have to wait until this yearly holiday in order to give thanks. We can thank God today, right now even. Let's share some things we're thankful for.

PRAY ABOUT IT

Dear God, we are thankful for You! We give thanks for all of the great blessings You have given to us. We thank You for helping us when we need it most. Amen.

God Wants Us to Be Grateful for Jesus

In everything give thanks. This is what God wants you to do because of Christ Jesus.

1 THESSALONIANS 5:18

TALK ABOUT IT

What are some things that you do or that we do as a family that show others just how grateful we are for Jesus?

READ ABOUT IT

Our family loves Jesus! It's important that we give thanks and show our gratitude for Jesus. Why? Because this will allow others to see just how special and important He really is to us. Going to church, attending Sunday school, participating in Vacation Bible School, going to church midweek, shows others that He is a priority to us. The best part is when we get to talk about Jesus with others or even invite them to come visit our church. Let's pray for God to show us other ways to express our gratefulness for Jesus.

PRAY ABOUT IT

Dear God, guide us in ways to let others know just how much Your Son, Jesus, means to us. Amen.

God Wants Us to Be Compassionate

God has chosen you. You are holy and loved by Him. Because of this, your new life should be full of loving-pity. You should be kind to others and have no pride. Be gentle and be willing to wait for others.

COLOSSIANS 3:12

TALK ABOUT IT

What are some ways that you show kindness toward others?

READ ABOUT IT

As your mommy, when I see you treating others with compassion it means so much to me. To be compassionate means that you are kind, gentle, tender, and able to put yourself in the shoes of another person. It's also important that we as a family show loving-kindness toward other families, including our neighbors. How about you pray with me for a loving heart? We can even ask God to show us how to love others.

PRAY ABOUT IT

Dear God, please give us a heart that is overflowing with Your compassion. Show us how we can love others the way that You have called us to. Amen.

God Wants Us to Be Patient

For it is not yet time for it to come true. The time is coming in a hurry, and it will come true. If you think it is slow in coming, wait for it. For it will happen for sure, and it will not wait.

HABAKKUK 2:3

TALK ABOUT IT

Tell me about a time when you were able to be patient.

READ ABOUT IT

Being patient isn't easy! As a mommy, I also find it hard to wait. The Bible says that when we wait, we can trust God is up to something good! It might take minutes, hours, days, weeks, months, or even years, but God is always doing great things for us. When we finally get to see something come true, it's great to look back and see how the waiting helped us.

PRAY ABOUT IT

Dear heavenly Daddy, thank You for the times we've had to just wait. It's not easy. There are things we are waiting for even now! Please give us Your patience. Amen.

God Wants Us to Give to Others

"In every way I showed you that by working hard like this we can help those who are weak. We must remember what the Lord Jesus said, 'We are more happy when we give than when we receive.'"

ACTS 20:35

TALK ABOUT IT

What are some ways that you have given to others?

READ ABOUT IT

It's so good to give to others. Giving is another way that God uses us to bless people. When we give, we don't need to always give a gift from the store. Sometimes it looks like our time, such as being there to help a friend or neighbor. Giving can also look like using your talents to help another person or teach them something. I'm proud of you when you give generously and don't expect anything in return.

PRAY ABOUT IT

Dear God, show us how we can be a blessing to others. Show us how to do this quietly and to not expect anything in return. Amen.

God Has Unlimited Power

*There is no one like You, O Lord. You are great,
and Your name is great in power.*

JEREMIAH 10:6

Talk about it

In order to be able to work properly, what items does our family own that require power?

Read about it

The lights in our rooms, our television, computer, refrigerator, microwave, toaster, and radio all need power. How do these items get their source of energy? They get plugged into an electrical outlet. Then the electricity comes through the power cord to supply these items with what they need, in order to turn on and function at their very best. God also has great power. When He lives in our hearts, we are tapping into the best power supply possible.

Pray about it

Dear God, we love you! When we forget about the power we have inside of us, please remind us that all we need is in You! Amen.

God Wants Us to Be a Blessing

God has given each of you a gift. Use it to help each other. This will show God's loving-favor.

1 PETER 4:10

TALK ABOUT IT

What do you think it means to be a blessing? What is one gift that you've used to bless another?

READ ABOUT IT

God has given all of us gifts. Some of us have athletic ability, which means we might be good at participating in a sport. Some of us have artistic abilities, which means we might be good at creative work like writing, singing, or playing music. And some of us have other talents and abilities. All of these things can be used for the glory of God to bless others. How? When you sing, it will brighten someone's day. When you play well in a sporting game and show good sportsmanship, it will inspire someone to do the same.

PRAY ABOUT IT

Dear God, use the gifts You have given us to share love with those around us. Amen.

God Wants Us to Slow Down

The Lord said, "I Myself will go with you.
I will give you rest."
EXODUS 33:14

TALK ABOUT IT

What are some of the things you like to do that help you calm down?

READ ABOUT IT

Getting a good night's sleep is very important for our body. It helps all of our muscles and organs to rest and recharge for another fun day. Sometimes when we don't feel well, we might need to rest more during the day than we normally do. This might require us to take a nap. The Bible says that it is important to slow down. It reminds you and me that we aren't God. We need to take a break from time to time and let Him take good care of us.

PRAY ABOUT IT

Dear God, thank You for giving us opportunities to rest. Thank You that You never rest so that we can entrust everything in Your hands while we slow down. Amen.

God Wants Us to Be Kind

You must be kind to each other. Think of the other person. Forgive other people just as God forgave you because of Christ's death on the cross.

EPHESIANS 4:32

TALK ABOUT IT

Share with me about a time you saw someone else be kind to another person.

READ ABOUT IT

Kindness is so important. When you are kind to me it makes me feel all warm and fuzzy inside. When we think of the other person, it is like a domino effect. One person is kind, then that person wants to be kind to another person, then another, and so on. It's a wonderful thing when we can be helpful, good, and gentle with others. When you and I do that, people have the chance to get a glimpse of God at work in our life and in theirs.

PRAY ABOUT IT

Dear Jesus, it's not easy to think of others. We ask for Your help in showing us how to be kind. Amen.

God Wants Us to Use Our Manners

"Do for other people whatever you would like to have them do for you. This is what the Jewish Law and the early preachers said."

MATTHEW 7:12

TALK ABOUT IT

Tell me about a time someone treated you the way you wanted to be treated. How did that make you feel?

READ ABOUT IT

I love it when you use your manners. It's as if you are treating me exactly how you'd like to be treated. Unfortunately, there will be times when people aren't nice to you. And sometimes you might forget to do the same. As your mommy, you've seen me make mistakes in this area too. When this happens, we can say we're sorry and do our best to turn the incident around for good.

PRAY ABOUT IT

Dear heavenly Daddy, ultimately You want us to treat others well. But sometimes we fall short and forget to use our manners. Help us to be respectful. When we aren't, help us to recognize it quickly. Amen.

God Wants Us to Be Polite

*Watch your talk! No bad words should be coming
from your mouth. Say what is good. Your words
should help others grow as Christians.*

EPHESIANS 4:29

TALK ABOUT IT

What has been one of the nicest things someone has ever said
to you?

READ ABOUT IT

Our words are powerful! They can help lift another person up
and brighten their day. Our words can also cause someone close
to us to feel less than their best or even discouraged. That's why
it's so important that we are careful with what we say and how
we say it and that we try to think before letting words come out
of our mouths. We want to tell the truth, but we don't want to
hurt someone's feelings.

PRAY ABOUT IT

Dear Jesus, You know what it was like to have bad things said
to You, and even *about* You. Help our words be polite toward
others. Amen.

God Wants Us to Have Fruit of the Spirit

But the fruit that comes from having the Holy Spirit in our lives is: love, joy, peace, not giving up, being kind, being good, having faith, being gentle, and being the boss over our own desires. The Law is not against these things.

GALATIANS 5:22-23

TALK ABOUT IT

What does it mean for us to have fruit in our lives?

READ ABOUT IT

The Bible uses the images of fruit to tell us a story. While we might have plenty of fruit in our kitchen and refrigerator, God also wants us to store spiritual fruit on the inside of us. This is so others can get to taste and see God's goodness on the outside of us through our words, actions, and daily living.

PRAY ABOUT IT

Dear God, may our lives have fruit—fruit that is delightful to those around us. Amen.

We Are a Part of God's Family

There are many people who belong to Christ.
And yet, we are one body which is Christ's.
We are all different but we depend on each other.

ROMANS 12:5

TALK ABOUT IT

Who is a part of our family? Who do you consider to be like family?

READ ABOUT IT

It's awesome that God has blessed us with family members! We get to learn so much from each other. I adore that you have unique talents and gifts that make you special. God has also blessed us with a church family. These are people that mean a lot to us and share the same values, and they are different from us too. Whether it's our family or our good friends from church, we all need each other and we all need God!

PRAY ABOUT IT

Dear God, thank You for family. We are so thankful to have a community of faith to call home. We are also thankful for the family in this home. Amen.

God Wants Us to Be Reliable

Whatever work you do, do it with all your heart.
Do it for the Lord and not for men.

COLOSSIANS 3:23

TALK ABOUT IT

What are some chores you do that help our family take good care of our home?

READ ABOUT IT

God created you and me to do many things. Work might not be fun all of the time, but it is necessary for us to do in order to get things done. Work can be fun, though, if it has purpose and meaning behind it. When we do things for God, our focus is on Him and not on others or how much we don't like doing something. Let's ask God to show us different ways we can be reliable children, so that His light shines through us.

PRAY ABOUT IT

Dear Jesus, we want to serve You well. Show us what we can do so people can experience Your grace in and through us. Amen.

God Wants Us to Serve

"If anyone wants to serve Me, he must follow Me.
So where I am, the one who wants to serve Me
will be there also. If anyone serves Me,
My Father will honor him."

JOHN 12:26

TALK ABOUT IT

What are some ways that you serve others? How do you serve God?

READ ABOUT IT

God wants us to focus on Him in all that we do. God also wants us to serve others. As we do, the focus isn't so that we get praised or rewarded for doing good things. God wants us to focus on serving for Him. When you do a nice job and don't expect anything in return, God sees that. He will honor you for doing great things because you cared more about praises from Him than from anyone else.

PRAY ABOUT IT

Dear God, when we serve others, help us to do so with a heart that is focused on You! Amen.

God Wants Us to Do What is Right

You have never been tempted to sin in any different way than other people. God is faithful. He will not allow you to be tempted more than you can take. But when you are tempted, He will make a way for you to keep from falling into sin.

1 CORINTHIANS 10:13

TALK ABOUT IT

What do you think the word *tempted* means?

READ ABOUT IT

When we are tempted, we are strongly drawn to do something that isn't the very best for us. God wants us to make the right choices, and He doesn't want us to sin. Thankfully, He understands that sometimes we don't make a good decision. When that happens, He will give us the opportunity to turn around and get back on the right path.

PRAY ABOUT IT

Dear God, when we feel tempted to do something that isn't right, please provide a way out so that we can get back on the path toward You. Amen.

God Wants Us to Forgive Others

Then Peter came to Jesus and said, "Lord, how many times may my brother sin against me and I forgive him, up to seven times?" Jesus said to him, "I tell you, not seven times but seventy times seven!"

MATTHEW 18:21-22

TALK ABOUT IT

When was the last time you had to forgive someone? What happened that caused you to forgive?

READ ABOUT IT

Forgiveness isn't easy. As your mommy, I've learned that it's a choice more than it's something that I want to do. Sometimes adults don't do a good job at saying we're sorry to each other. When this happens, I've had to choose to forgive anyway. That frees me up to be who God wants me to be. It helps me to not think about or be angry over the situation but to trust that God knows.

PRAY ABOUT IT

Dear God, help us to forgive those who have hurt us so that we can live in Your freedom. Amen.

God Created Seasons

*"While the earth lasts, planting time and gathering
time, cold and heat, summer and winter,
and day and night will not end."*

GENESIS 8:22

Talk about it

What are some activities that you like to do during the fall, winter, spring, and summer months? Which of the four seasons is your favorite?

Read about it

There are so many neat things to do throughout the calendar year. It has been fun to be able to create some traditions with you and our family and make memories. God created so much for us, including the seasons. He tells the clouds when to rain, thunder, or snow. He tells the flowers when to blossom and the trees when to let their leaves fall to the ground.

Pray about it

Dear Creator, You are so amazing! How are You able to make everything? It's too much for us to understand. We are just so grateful to be able to enjoy what You've made with Your hands! Amen.

God Wants Us to Be Born Again

For if a man belongs to Christ, he is a new person.
The old life is gone. New life has begun.

2 CORINTHIANS 5:17

TALK ABOUT IT

What do you think it means to be born again?

READ ABOUT IT

You have a birthday, the day when you were born into this world as a new baby. It's a day that we celebrate. As your mommy, on this day I remember how you came into this world. You are a blessing that changed my life forever! I can't imagine life without you! As a child of God, we also like to remember when we put our faith in Jesus. In fact, it's another great day for celebration! The Bible often refers to this as being born again because you are birthed into the faith.

PRAY ABOUT IT

Dear Jesus, thank You for dying on the cross so that we can be forgiven. We accept You into our lives. Amen.

God Wants Us to Be Content

Keep your lives free from the love of money.
Be happy with what you have. God has said,
"I will never leave you or let you be alone."

HEBREWS 13:5

TALK ABOUT IT

Content is a big word. What do you think it means?

READ ABOUT IT

Content is a word that helps describe the state of who we are. It is wanting nothing more or nothing less. It is being appreciative for what we have. It's not simple to be at ease with what we have, though. Sometimes you and I might see a friend has something or has achieved something that leaves us wanting more in life. But God wants us to be okay with who we are. Because in God's eyes, you and I are already enough. And so is He.

PRAY ABOUT IT

Dear God, help us to know what it means to truly want nothing more and nothing less. Help us to believe that You are truly enough for us. Amen.

God Knows the Stars

He knows the number of the stars.
He gives names to all of them.

PSALM 147:4

TALK ABOUT IT

When you look up at the sky and see the stars, what do you think about? How many days do you think it would take to travel to one?

READ ABOUT IT

God not only knows the number of hairs on your head, He also knows how many stars are in the sky as well as their names! Just like God created you and me, He also created them. I just love being able to look up at them with you. It's so fun to see the stars and think about how far away they are. Wouldn't it be cool to ride on a rocket ship just to get up close to one?

PRAY ABOUT IT

Dear God, You created everything! It's so awesome to look all around us and see Your hand at work in creation. Amen.

God Wants Us to Be Agents of Peace

As much as you can, live in peace with all men.

ROMANS 12:18

TALK ABOUT IT

What do you think it means to be an agent of peace?

READ ABOUT IT

An agent is someone who has the power to act. Therefore, an agent of peace is someone who has the power to act peacefully. As children of God, we can choose to be the type of people who want to be peaceful. I know this isn't easy, but with God's help in our lives it can be done. How? By praying for His calming presence during those times when all we want to do is yell, scream, or fight.

PRAY ABOUT IT

Dear God, when we want to act out please help us to remain still. Please give us the calmness we need throughout the day so that Your peace flows right through us. Amen.

God Wants Us to Speak Up

I am not ashamed of the Good News. It is the power of God. It is the way He saves men from the punishment of their sins if they put their trust in Him. It is for the Jew first and for all other people also.

ROMANS 1:16

TALK ABOUT IT

What is it like to share about Jesus with someone you know or don't know?

READ ABOUT IT

Talking with others about what you believe in can feel a little bit scary. As a mommy, it's not always easy for me to talk about Jesus too. But when God has provided the opportunity for me to do so, I get so excited. Joy bubbles up from the inside of me to the point I can't contain it! I do believe that God will always honor the moments you get to share about Him with others. There's no need to be afraid.

PRAY ABOUT IT

Dear God, please give us the boldness to speak about You. Amen.

God Wants Us to Play

Sing to Him a new song.
Play well with loud sounds of joy.

PSALM 33:3

TALK ABOUT IT

What are some things you like to do for celebration or to express joy?

READ ABOUT IT

There are many different ways that you and I can play. Sometimes we play house, other times a game, or maybe we get to play in a swimming pool! Sometimes you have friends that come over to play. It's so fun to hear someone play their instrument too. All of these different varieties of play are important. Playfulness is fun and it allows us to express ourselves. As children of God, expressing ourselves with good play is a way that honors God and is pleasing to Him.

PRAY ABOUT IT

Dear God, when we play please help us to do so in a way that glorifies You! Help us to have fun and let Your light shine through us. Amen.

God Has a Purpose for You

"For I know the plans I have for you," says the Lord,
"plans for well-being and not for trouble,
to give you a future and a hope."

JEREMIAH 29:11

TALK ABOUT IT

What do you believe is your purpose in life?

READ ABOUT IT

God has a purpose for you, little one. Even at your young age He has some special things for you to do. Whether it's being in school, at home, or activities outside of the house, you can do everything with a sense of purpose. When you do everything with God in mind, He will show you who to help, who to love, and how to be a blessing. In turn, this will provide the chance for you to share about what you believe in.

PRAY ABOUT IT

Dear God, please open doors of opportunity for us to live with Your purpose and meaning in all that we say and do. Amen.

God Stays the Same

*Jesus Christ is the same yesterday
and today and forever.*

HEBREWS 13:8

TALK ABOUT IT

How is it that something that is many, many, many years old can still be the same?

READ ABOUT IT

Jesus Christ is God's Son. They have been around since the beginning of creation, and even before that! Even though they have been around forever, they are still the same today. How can that be? Because all of the promises found in God's Word are still true for you and me. We might change; we might go off and make our own decisions separate from what God might want us to do, but God has always been there for us.

PRAY ABOUT IT

Dear Jesus, it's so hard for us to understand how You can still be the same today. But we trust that You haven't changed one bit. Amen.

God Shows Loving-Kindness

But God had so much loving-kindness.
He loved us with such a great love.

EPHESIANS 2:4

TALK ABOUT IT

In reading through these devotionals together, what have you learned so far about God's love for us?

READ ABOUT IT

We don't deserve it, but because God loves us so very much we get to benefit from His mercy. God looks upon us with loving-kindness. He has compassion for us and a genuine affection for His children that can't be explained. As your mom, I don't know if I'll ever fully grasp the endless grace and mercy of God that is in my life. But I know it's there, and I can think of several times I've seen it displayed clearly for me to see.

PRAY ABOUT IT

Dear God, we cannot comprehend Your great love for us. A love that includes mercy and loving-kindness that is endless. Wow! Amen.

God Knows Your Hair

"God knows how many hairs you have on your head. Do not be afraid. You are worth more than many small birds."

LUKE 12:7

Talk about it

How many hairs do you think are on my head? How about yours?

Read about it

We have a lot of hair on our head! Some people have long hair, some short. Some people have curly hair, some straight or wavy. Some people have red, blond, brown, black, or dyed hair. No matter what the dressing on top of you, God knows exactly what it looks like and how many hairs are on there. Isn't that awesome? We could never actually count all our strands, but God does. That tells us something: God knows *everything* about us!

Pray about it

Dear God, we think it's pretty cool that You know so many details about us. Thank You for being in charge of our lives. Amen.

God Is Our Greatest Encourager

"Have I not told you? Be strong and have strength of heart! Do not be afraid or lose faith. For the Lord your God is with you anywhere you go."

JOSHUA 1:9

TALK ABOUT IT

Who is your greatest encourager? What is it about them that makes them an encourager?

READ ABOUT IT

When you and I think about all of the people who have encouraged or praised us, we might be reminded of the things they said or did to show us their support. God is our greatest encourager. Over and over again in the Bible, He tells us to not be afraid or lose faith. He reminds us that He is always with us.

PRAY ABOUT IT

Dear God, thank You for always being with us! We are so grateful that You are our biggest fan! Help us to keep our eyes fixed on You! Amen.

God Is Holy

One called out to another and said, "Holy, holy, holy, is the Lord of All. The whole earth is full of His shining-greatness."

ISAIAH 6:3

TALK ABOUT IT

What do you think it means to be holy?

READ ABOUT IT

When something is holy it is considered to have a spiritually pure quality. Often it is a word used to describe someone that is devoted to the service of God. God is holy because He is the very nature and foundation of what it means to be holy. Another way to describe something that is holy is for it to be set apart. As your mommy, I pray that I would be set apart. That I would guide and parent you in a way that follows God, not what might be considered popular or likable.

PRAY ABOUT IT

Dear Jesus, help us to be like You. Although we aren't perfect, we trust that You can help us do the best that we can with what You have given us. Amen.

You Are a Child of God

He gave the right and the power to become children of God to those who received Him. He gave this to those who put their trust in His name.

JOHN 1:12

Talk about it

What do you like most about being young?

Read about it

You are my child, and I am a child to my mommy. Because you and I trust and have faith in our heavenly Daddy we are also His children. So even though I'm older than you, I'm still a child in God's eyes. And someday when you are grown up, you will still be my child and most importantly God's. Pretty cool, huh?

Pray about it

Dear heavenly Daddy, we give thanks for being Yours. Because of this promise we are free to be who You created us to be! Amen.

God Is Our Father

There is one God. He is the Father of us all.
He is over us all. He is the One working
through us all. He is the One living in us all.

EPHESIANS 4:6

TALK ABOUT IT

What do you love the most about Daddy, Grandpa, or your uncle?

READ ABOUT IT

If you were to take all of the great and awesome qualities of the most important men in your life and place them into one individual, that would be a pretty spectacular person! God is so much to us; He is our Father on earth and in heaven. God created you inside of me. He cares for you in a way that is wonderful and miraculous. He showers you with His love and affection every day.

PRAY ABOUT IT

Dear Father, there is so much to love about You! Thank You for creating us and for ruling over our lives. Amen.

God Is Indescribable

The Holy Writings say, "No eye has ever seen or no ear has ever heard or no mind has ever thought of the wonderful things God has made ready for those who love Him."
1 CORINTHIANS 2:9

TALK ABOUT IT

What are some of the awesome and wonderful things that God has made in this world?

READ ABOUT IT

When you and I go outside to play, go for a walk to the park, or take a bike ride, we get to see some amazing stuff! Depending upon what time of the year it is we might see trees budding or losing their leaves, flowers blooming, green grass growing, animals running around, and so much more! God made everything we see and it's so much fun to experience it with you! How about sometime soon we go on a nature walk and tell each other about the great things we see that God made for us to enjoy?

PRAY ABOUT IT

Dear God, thank You for making everything! Amen.

God Rewards

*A man cannot please God unless he has faith.
Anyone who comes to God must believe that He
is. That one must also know that God gives what is
promised to the one who keeps on looking for Him.*

Hebrews 11:6

Talk about it

Tell me about a time you received an award. What did you need to do in order to get it?

Read about it

It's such a great feeling to be rewarded for good work. Sometimes you have to work really, really hard or study a lot, in order to see great results. When we follow God and live by faith, that pleases Him. As we stay on track and do what needs to be done, God will reward us. He will give us what has been promised.

Pray about it

Dear God, as we do our part to live by faith, we will trust that You see us and will reward us. Amen.

God Is Powerful

He is your praise and He is your God. You have seen the great and powerful things He has done for you.

DEUTERONOMY 10:21

TALK ABOUT IT

What does it mean that God is powerful?

READ ABOUT IT

God has the ability to do anything. *Anything!* As we read about Him in the Bible, we realize that there's nothing He can't do. So if He's so powerful, why doesn't He do anything we want? Well, God is good to us. He doesn't want to give us everything we ask for. He wants to give us what we need and what is best. Which means He wants to demonstrate His power in our lives in a way that works best with His will for us.

PRAY ABOUT IT

Dear God, it's awesome that You are so powerful! Help us to tap into Your power not for our own benefit but for Yours! Amen.

God Is Gracious

The Lord is loving and right. Yes,
our God is full of loving-kindness.
PSALM 116:5

TALK ABOUT IT

What have you learned so far about God's grace toward us?

READ ABOUT IT

Grace means that we get what we don't deserve. And we get these things because God is full of loving-kindness toward you and me. As we've learned in previous devotions, this means He has compassion for us and a deep affection. He is gentle, tender, and patient with us. As your mommy, I'm so grateful for God's grace because every day I make mistakes. It's God's undeserved favor that helps to turn my shortcomings around for good.

PRAY ABOUT IT

Dear God, we are so amazed by Your great grace! There are a lot of things we have and experiences we've shared that are because of who You are to us. Amen.

God Is Just

I know that the Lord will stand by those who suffer and do what is right for the poor.

PSALM 140:12

TALK ABOUT IT

What is it like to see people who are going through a hard time? What do you do when you feel sad?

READ ABOUT IT

Life isn't fair all the time. In fact the Bible talks about how there will be troubles in this life. So what do we do when we see someone who is going through a hard time? What do we do when we are sad? We go to God. We can help show someone the love of God through our actions or offering to pray for them. We can pray for help. Jesus says for us to take heart because He has overcome the world.

PRAY ABOUT IT

Dear God, we trust that no matter what we face You are always there with us. Amen.

God Is Enough

God can give you all you need. He will give you more than enough. You will have everything you need for yourselves. And you will have enough left over to give when there is a need.

2 CORINTHIANS 9:8

TALK ABOUT IT

What do you think it means when I say that God is enough for us?

READ ABOUT IT

Want. Want. Want. Sometimes all we want is what we want! Whether it's a toy or a yummy food item, there is a lot we would like to have but don't need. God knows what is best for us. In fact, when you and I keep our eyes on Him, we will find that He's enough. Because God made everything, we can learn the art of being at peace with what we have and even with what we don't have.

PRAY ABOUT IT

Dear heavenly Daddy, You are enough for us. We thank You for everything You have given us including this time together with each other! Amen.

God Is on Time

Wait for the Lord. Be strong. Let your heart be strong. Yes, wait for the Lord.

PSALM 27:14

TALK ABOUT IT

What is it like to make it to school, practice, or some other appointment and you're not late, you're not even early, but you're right on time?

READ ABOUT IT

The God you and I believe in is always on time. When you are waiting for a prayer to be answered, He hears you and will grant your request—as long as it's a part of His will for you. As you grow up, you might feel impatient or worry if God will ever show up and answer your prayers. He will, dear child. He will.

PRAY ABOUT IT

Dear God, when we feel impatient or start to worry, please help us to trust You. Help us to remember the moments that You weren't too early or too late. You are always on time! Amen.

God Has a Helper

"The Helper is the Holy Spirit. The Father will send Him in My place. He will teach you everything and help you remember everything I have told you."

JOHN 14:26

TALK ABOUT IT

Who do you think is God's helper? What is He like?

READ ABOUT IT

When Jesus was about to leave this world, He told people that a Helper would stay behind. If Jesus didn't go to heaven, this Helper wouldn't be here on earth within us. Who is this? The Holy Spirit! The Holy Spirit lives inside of you and me. When we pray to God and ask for assistance, the Holy Spirit is who guides us.

PRAY ABOUT IT

Dear Jesus, thank You for coming into this world. Thank You for all that You did while You were here. Thank You that after You left You gave us the Holy Spirit to live inside of us. Amen.

God Gives Fruit

"I am the Vine and you are the branches. Get your life from Me. Then I will live in you and you will give much fruit. You can do nothing without Me."

JOHN 15:5

Talk about it

There are a lot of fruit that come from trees. Which fruit(s) do you like and why?

Read about it

There are so many different varieties of apples to choose from. Some are sweet, some are tart, and some are bittersweet. Some apples are big, some are tiny, some are red, golden, or green. Each has its own unique qualities. When Jesus lives in our hearts, we—like an apple tree—get to bear fruit. We don't get to produce fruit to eat, or for others to munch on. This fruit comes in the form of love, joy, peace, patience, kindness, goodness, faithfulness, gentleness, and self-control.

Pray about it

Dear God, we love that we get to partner with You in producing faith-filled fruit in this world. Amen.

God Is Real

Men cannot say they do not know about God. From the beginning of the world, men could see what God is like through the things He has made. This shows His power that lasts forever. It shows that He is God.

ROMANS 1:20

TALK ABOUT IT

What are some things that have happened in your life that show you God is real?

READ ABOUT IT

When you and I hear about bad things happening in this world, we might wonder if God is real. When you and I see good and beauty, we are reminded that God is real. So how do we come to terms with the fact that God is real in the good and the bad? We trust Him. We hold on to our faith like we hold on to a blanket or stuffed animal. We believe that even good can come from hard situations.

PRAY ABOUT IT

Dear God, You are real to us! As we read this devotion, we believe that You are here. Amen.

God Is Hidden

*Then they will cry to the Lord, but He will not answer
them. He will hide His face from them at that time,
because they have done sinful things.*

MICAH 3:4

TALK ABOUT IT

Do you think that God is really hidden? What does our sin do
to us and God?

READ ABOUT IT

Sweetheart, when you and I do something that we know we
shouldn't do and it hurts us or someone else, it is called sin.
When we sin, we distance ourselves from the very best that
God has for us. In those moments that we feel the gap between
us and God, it may seem like He is hiding from us. What really
happens is we are distancing ourselves from God. When we seek
God and confess that what we did was wrong, then we get to
see Him more clearly once more.

PRAY ABOUT IT

Dear God, we want to see You! When we make a mistake, help
us to quickly apologize to You. Amen.

God's Love Is Perfect

No person has ever seen God at any time.
If we love each other, God lives in us.
His love is made perfect in us.

1 JOHN 4:12

TALK ABOUT IT

What do you think perfect love means?

READ ABOUT IT

Is there such a thing as perfect love? I don't know if there is. But if God lives in our hearts, we will have the chance to experience this type of deep compassion and affection for each other. We may not always express it, but there's a chance we will get to become a mirror image of what it means to be loving. If a person we care about also has God in their hearts, then that makes it possible for us to experience God's perfect love, together.

PRAY ABOUT IT

Dear God, it's hard to think about what it must be like to let Your love be made perfect in us. Help us to be like You, so that we can experience it. Amen.

God Shows Us Favor

Let the favor of the Lord our God be upon us.
And make the work of our hands stand strong.
Yes, make the work of our hands stand strong.

PSALM 90:17

TALK ABOUT IT

What does favor mean?

READ ABOUT IT

When something is done or granted out of goodwill, is a kind act or friendly, that is considered favor. God gives us these blessings every single day! He is so good and gracious to us. He uses the people in our lives to show us His loving-kindness. The Bible says He's always with us, watching over us—no matter what! I'm so grateful that we love a God who showers His blessings and goodwill upon us all the time.

PRAY ABOUT IT

Dear God, You are awesome! We pray to be more aware of Your favor every day of our lives. May everything we do remind us that Your mighty hand is upon us. Amen.

God Doesn't Want Us to Be Afraid

In God I have put my trust. I will not be afraid.
What can man do to me?

PSALM 56:11

TALK ABOUT IT

What makes you feel afraid?

READ ABOUT IT

There are a lot of things in this world that can make us feel afraid. Whether it's a dark room, being in an unfamiliar place, riding on a roller coaster, or seeing a big hairy spider, all of these things can frighten us. But you know what? God's Word tells us that we can trust Him. When we do, we can tell Him all about our fears. As we tell Him our concerns and remind ourselves of our faith in Him, we can remember that He's with us. We don't need to be afraid anymore.

PRAY ABOUT IT

Dear God, we admit that there's a lot that causes us to feel scared. We ask that You would take these feelings and replace them with faith in You. Amen.

God Is Wise

In Christ are hidden all the riches
of wisdom and understanding.

COLOSSIANS 2:3

TALK ABOUT IT

What does it mean to be wise? Can you share with me an example of when you were wise?

READ ABOUT IT

To be wise is to have the ability to know right from wrong or to have an understanding for something. God the Father and Jesus are the ones who are the wisest of all. When you and I need help figuring out what is right or wrong, or we need more faith knowledge, God is the one we can turn to. All we need to do is ask Him for help and He will provide it.

PRAY ABOUT IT

Dear Jesus, help us to not be wise in our own minds but wise because we asked You for help. Amen.

We Can Run with God

All these many people who have had faith in God are around us like a cloud. Let us put every thing out of our lives that keeps us from doing what we should. Let us keep running in the race that God has planned for us.

Hebrews 12:1

Talk about it

What activities or sports do you enjoy participating in? Why do you enjoy them so much?

Read about it

The Bible compares running a race to living our lives for Jesus. A faith-filled life isn't always easy, but it is the best! It requires commitment, obedience, and sometimes we might feel like we just want to give up. The Bible verse we read is meant to encourage us to keep going, have fun, and stay focused on God.

Pray about it

Dear God, help us to look toward You in all that we do. We love this time together reading and praying because it strengthens our faith. Amen.

God Is Great

Great is our Lord, and great in power.
His understanding has no end.

PSALM 147:5

TALK ABOUT IT

Share with me a time that you got to experience God's greatness. Was it at church, at home, or somewhere else? What happened?

READ ABOUT IT

I love sharing with you about the times when we have experienced the greatness of God. Sometimes we get to see His greatness in a sunrise or sunset. Sometimes we experience it when we see an answer to prayer. Other times we see just how awesome He is in these moments, like reading this devotional together. His greatness is all around us including the love of our family, church community, neighborhood, and friends.

PRAY ABOUT IT

Dear God, we're so grateful for the awesome things You have done in our lives! Sometimes big experiences and sometimes small—either way You are enough for us! Amen.

God Knows Everything

You know when I sit down and when I get up.
You understand my thoughts from far away.

PSALM 139:2

TALK ABOUT IT

In what ways have you seen that God truly knows everything about you?

READ ABOUT IT

God knows everything about you, little one. He even knows everything about me! I'm in awe of the fact that God knows so much about every single person on the earth! How is this true? I've seen Him answer our prayers. I've watched Him provide for our needs as a family. I've witnessed unexpected blessings. I've seen Him bless me with people like you, which has allowed for me to better understand His love for us.

PRAY ABOUT IT

Dear God, we're so thankful that You know all of the details about us. Right now, You are holding us in the palm of Your hand, which makes us happy to be called Your children. Amen.

Jesus Read

Jesus came to Nazareth where He had grown up.
As He had done before, He went into the Jewish
place of worship on the Day of Rest.
Then He stood up to read.

LUKE 4:16

TALK ABOUT IT

What do you like to read? What do you think Jesus liked to read?

READ ABOUT IT

I really enjoy spending this time with you. We get to read God's Word, we get to talk about it, and we get to pray together. This is such a fun way to encourage and develop an important habit of daily time with God. Like Jesus did when He read, we get to explore simple truths of scripture and relate them to everyday life.

PRAY ABOUT IT

Dear God, thank You for giving us the gift of reading! If we didn't have the ability to do so, we wouldn't be able to have this time together and with You! Amen.

God Is Everywhere

*But for sure, as I live, all the earth will be filled
with the shining-greatness of the Lord.*

NUMBERS 14:21

TALK ABOUT IT

When you and I are outside, or inside, what gives you proof that
God is truly everywhere?

READ ABOUT IT

Since God created everything He is also everywhere! He's right
here with us as we read the words on this page. He is in our home
and outside of our house. He's with you at school or when you
play with a friend. He's on the bus, in the car, and at the gym.
He's in your room and the places you walk around. He has filled
everything on this earth with His goodness and greatness. When
we travel far from home, He's there too.

PRAY ABOUT IT

Dear God, thank You for the reminder that You are always with
us. Thank You for being everywhere! Amen.

God Is in Control of the Earth

For God is the King of all the earth.
Sing praises with a well written song.

PSALM 47:7

TALK ABOUT IT

What do you think it means that God is in control of the earth?

READ ABOUT IT

God is in control of us and this whole entire world! This means that He is the One who is commanding this planet to go around the sun. He gives direction and dominates over every living creature. God is King! Because we have a loving Father who is on the throne in heaven and who watches over us, we can give thanks. Another way to express our thanksgiving is to sing praises. Let's do that!

PRAY ABOUT IT

Dear God, we praise You! We thank You for being in complete and total control of our lives. We praise You for giving us this time together. Amen.

God Gives Us Strength

He answered me, "I am all you need. I give you My
loving-favor. My power works best in weak people."
I am happy to be weak and have troubles
so I can have Christ's power in me.

2 CORINTHIANS 12:9

Talk about it

When you are feeling down or upset, what do you like to do that makes you feel better?

Read about it

Think about a time when you weren't feeling good. Maybe you were sick, or you were upset about something. When we don't feel our best, we often feel weak. Scripture says that when we feel this way we are actually strong. When you and I turn our focus away from what is bothering us and think about Jesus, we will find strength. When we pray to Him and ask for His help, He will give it to us.

Pray about it

Dear God, when I don't feel at my best, help me to remember You are my strength. Amen.

God Is Our Banner

*Moses built an altar and gave it the
name The Lord is My Banner.*

EXODUS 17:15

TALK ABOUT IT

What do you think it means that the Lord is our Banner?

READ ABOUT IT

When you and I see a banner hanging outside of a store, on a flagpole, at a sporting event, or outside a home—or on special holidays like the Fourth of July—it symbolizes something. That *something* is unity and an identity. When you and I say that the Lord is our Banner, He symbolizes unity in our faith in Him. God also gives us an identity that can only be found in Him.

PRAY ABOUT IT

Dear God, You are so many things to us. Thank You for being our Banner. A Banner that we can raise up high with our hands, our voices, through our actions, through our gifts and service. Amen.

God's Word Is Alive

God's Word is living and powerful. It is sharper than a sword that cuts both ways. It cuts straight into where the soul and spirit meet and it divides them. It cuts into the joints and bones. It tells what the heart is thinking about and what it wants to do.

HEBREWS 4:12

TALK ABOUT IT

How can it be that God's Word, the Bible, is truly alive?

READ ABOUT IT

When you and I read the Bible we will find that what it has to say is important in our daily lives, just as much as it was when it was written many years ago. We might be going through a hard time. Suddenly, what we are reading in the Bible stands out to us. We realize it speaks to exactly what we are going through and encourages us. That's how it becomes alive in us!

PRAY ABOUT IT

Dear God, thank You that Your Word is still powerful! We're grateful that it speaks to us even today. Amen.

God Restores

After you have suffered for awhile, God Himself will
make you perfect. He will keep you in the right way.
He will give you strength. He is the God of all loving-
favor and has called you through Christ Jesus
to share His shining-greatness forever.

1 PETER 5:10

TALK ABOUT IT

Share with me about a time you saw God restore you. Were
you sick and you got better? Were you sad and by the end of
the day happy?

READ ABOUT IT

There are things in life that just happen. We might get sick and
have to miss school or a friend moves away or we don't do well
on a test. It can be hard to see God's goodness in all of it. Yet,
through every hard thing, God always has something good on
the other side. He is a God who promises to help us!

PRAY ABOUT IT

Dear Jesus, thank You for lifting us up and restoring us when
we need it. Amen.

God Gives Us Rest

*"Come to Me, all of you who work and
have heavy loads. I will give you rest."*
MATTHEW 11:28

TALK ABOUT IT

What are some of your favorite ways to rest?

READ ABOUT IT

There are a lot of things that you and I do throughout the day.
We work, we play, we go to school, and we do chores. Sometimes
you have practice, a lesson, or other activity. Sometimes I like to
get some exercise. By the end of the day we can feel tired. I'm so
thankful that God created us to rest! Without it we'd just keep
going and going and be so worn out. Rest helps us to continue
to enjoy the things we do together.

PRAY ABOUT IT

Dear heavenly Daddy, we're so grateful that You created us to be
able to rest. Thank You that You do not stop working. This way,
when we rest we can entrust everything to You. Amen.

God Provides Everything

The Lord is my Shepherd.
I will have everything I need.

PSALM 23:1

TALK ABOUT IT

What ways have you seen God provide for everything you need?

READ ABOUT IT

Look around us. As we sit here and read this devotional, we can see that God has already provided for many of our needs. He's blessed us with this time together, a home, furniture, food, warmth, light, and so much more! As your mommy, I can go on and on about how I've witnessed our needs being met in this family, even during some of the most challenging seasons. We most certainly do have everything we need, even many of our wants.

PRAY ABOUT IT

Gracious God, we are so blessed to have all that You have given us. May we continue to have the eyes to see that You always provide us with everything that we need. Amen.

Jesus Was Born in Bethlehem

Jesus was born in the town of Bethlehem in the country of Judea. It was the time when Herod was king of that part of the country. Soon after Jesus was born, some wise men who learned things from stars came to Jerusalem from the East.

MATTHEW 2:1

TALK ABOUT IT

What city and state were you born in?

READ ABOUT IT

I remember the day you were born. Oh you brought so much joy into my life! You were such a blessing to our family. People came to visit us at the hospital. They wanted to see you, hold you, and give you gifts. We took pictures of you to help us remember that precious day. The days following your birth, there were even more friends and family who came over to visit us. They especially wanted to meet you! I'm so grateful to have you in my life!

PRAY ABOUT IT

Dear God, thank You for blessing us with each other. Amen.

Jesus Has a Birthday

Today, One Who saves from the punishment of sin has been born in the city of David. He is Christ the Lord.

LUKE 2:11

Talk about it

What do you think it was like to celebrate Jesus' first birthday?

Read about it

We celebrate the birth of Jesus on Christmas Day. You and I also have a special day called our birthday. Like we do at Christmastime when we remember Jesus and His birth, I love being able to reflect on and remember your special day. You came into this world and changed my life for the better—forever! You also have been such a blessing to so many other people in our family. If we invite Jesus to make a home in our hearts, He will also change and bless our lives.

Pray about it

Dear Jesus, we love celebrating You! Help us to remember that Your birthday isn't just about giving or getting gifts. It's also about remembering just how special You are to us! Amen.

Jesus Died and Rose

Christ suffered and died for sins once for all.
He never sinned and yet He died for us who have
sinned. He died so He might bring us to God.
His body died but His spirit was made alive.

1 PETER 3:18

TALK ABOUT IT

What does it mean that Jesus died and rose again?

READ ABOUT IT

Jesus died on a cross, was buried, and three days later He rose again. The act of dying and rising is also known as resurrection; it is rising again from decay. A great example of this is a flower. It starts out as a seed in the dirt and eventually rises above the ground to blossom. Jesus did this in our lives so that you and I can find freedom and forgiveness for our sins.

PRAY ABOUT IT

Dear Jesus, we are so grateful for the example You became for us here on earth. You were so willing to lay down your life so that we can blossom in You. Amen.

Jesus Is Risen

"He is not here! He has risen from the dead
as He said He would. Come and see
the place where the Lord lay."

MATTHEW 28:6

TALK ABOUT IT

What are some of your favorite ways to celebrate that Jesus is risen?

READ ABOUT IT

Easter is such a great holiday! I love celebrating it with you and our family. We get to enjoy candy, decorate Easter eggs, have an Easter egg hunt, and eat lots of yummy foods. We also go to church, perhaps wear a new spring outfit, and get to see flowers start to blossom. Most important of all, we get to remember what Jesus did on the cross. He died, was buried, and three days later He rose again! Now we get to proclaim that He is our risen Savior.

PRAY ABOUT IT

Dear Jesus, it's so awesome that You are risen! What a wonderful Savior and friend we have in You! Amen.

God Set Us Apart

Do not act like the sinful people of the world. Let God change your life. First of all, let Him give you a new mind. Then you will know what God wants you to do. And the things you do will be good and pleasing and perfect.

ROMANS 12:2

TALK ABOUT IT

What does it mean that God set you and me apart?

READ ABOUT IT

You and I are not perfect, but because of Jesus, we are His children. As we remain dedicated and devoted to God, that is how we become more and more set apart. It seems as though there might be a lot we have to do to earn this, but we don't. We just need to continually recognize that He's God and we're not, and that we need His forgiveness every day.

PRAY ABOUT IT

Dear heavenly Daddy, we don't deserve Your goodness toward us. We don't deserve to be considered set apart in Your eyes, but we are! Thank You! Amen.

God Fills Us

I pray that you will know the love of Christ. His love goes beyond anything we can understand. I pray that you will be filled with God Himself.

EPHESIANS 3:19

TALK ABOUT IT

What do you think it means that you will be filled with God Himself?

READ ABOUT IT

The scripture we just read is a beautiful prayer that talks about the love of Christ. That Jesus' love would be something we know about and experience. His love is so big and awesome that it's often hard to fully understand how we would be filled with God Himself. In a way, this invites us to be overflowing with Christ's love so that we would be filled to the very top of our heads and the bottoms of our feet with God's goodness.

PRAY ABOUT IT

Dear Jesus, may Your love flow through us so that others get to experience the goodness found in You! Amen.

God Is Before Us

*You have closed me in from behind and in front.
And You have laid Your hand upon me.*

PSALM 139:5

TALK ABOUT IT

What are some examples that show you God is in front of you and behind you?

READ ABOUT IT

Think back to a time when you were playing and if you made one wrong move you would have gotten hurt really badly. Or what about a time that if you made a poor choice you would have gotten into a lot of trouble. Or maybe a time you took a test and if you got one more question wrong you wouldn't have gotten a good grade. In those moments, God was with you. He was behind you and before you, making sure you were okay as He provided a good outcome.

PRAY ABOUT IT

Dear God, thank You for watching over us. Thank You for protecting us. Amen.

God Is Beautiful

God shines from Zion, perfect in beauty.

PSALM 50:2

TALK ABOUT IT

What are some items that you consider to be beautiful? Why are they pretty to you?

READ ABOUT IT

You, my child, are beautiful! Everything about you is amazing and very special to me. God blessed me when He put you into my life. From the way you smile and laugh, to how you show love and care for others. You are beautiful from the inside and out! God made you and He is also beautiful. Everything He creates is awesome! When He lives in our hearts, we will also shine like Him. The Bible says we can live clean lives that allow us to shine like bright lights in this world.

PRAY ABOUT IT

Dear God, all that we see is a reflection of You and Your creation. Thank You for the beauty that radiates throughout the world. Amen.

God Has Armor for Us to Wear

This is the last thing I want to say:
Be strong with the Lord's strength.

EPHESIANS 6:10

Talk about it

When you play dress up or pretend, what do you like to put on?

Read about it

The Bible says that we are to be strong in the Lord's strength. What does this look like? A man named Paul tells us what this means. During his day, a Roman soldier wore armor. This armor helped protect the soldier and gave him strength. In the same way, you and I can put on these pretend clothes. But this armor reminds us of God and our faith in Him. Let's stand up and put it on together. (Read more in Ephesians 6:14–17.)

Pray about it

Dear heavenly Daddy, our strength comes from You! We love putting on Your wardrobe because it reminds us of the dependence we have in You! Amen.

The Holy Spirit Helps Us Pray

In the same way, the Holy Spirit helps us where we are weak. We do not know how to pray or what we should pray for, but the Holy Spirit prays to God for us with sounds that cannot be put into words.

ROMANS 8:26

TALK ABOUT IT

What is your favorite way to pray to God?

READ ABOUT IT

There are many different ways to praise and talk to God. You and I can go for a walk and pray out loud. We can use our words with God silently, on our knees, or standing up. We can talk to God, sing, and even shout. And God loves them all because He wants to hear from us. When we don't know what to say, we can ask the Holy Spirit for help. He'll show us the way.

PRAY ABOUT IT

Dear God, thank You for giving us the gift of the Holy Spirit. May Your Spirit show us how to pray. Amen.

God Put Forever in Us

He has made everything beautiful in its time.
He has put thoughts of the forever in man's mind,
yet man cannot understand the work God has
done from the beginning to the end.

ECCLESIASTES 3:11

TALK ABOUT IT

If you could live forever, what would you like to do?

READ ABOUT IT

None of us want to say goodbye to this world. Leaving our family, friends, and toys behind isn't a fun thing to think about. Our bodies aren't meant to live forever on this side of heaven though. When we put our faith, hope, and trust in Jesus as our Savior, then we will get to live with Him forever after we leave earth. God created us. He put the desire to keep on living in our hearts—and with Him, we will.

PRAY ABOUT IT

Dear God, we thank You for putting the thoughts of forever in our hearts. We look forward to continuing to live with You in eternity. Amen.

God Created Us

*I will give thanks to You, for the greatness of the way
I was made brings fear. Your works are great
and my soul knows it very well.*

PSALM 139:14

TALK ABOUT IT

What are some of the things that you really like about yourself?

READ ABOUT IT

I love everything about you! I give thanks to God for you! Why?
Because He created you. He created you right inside of me. I
was also created right inside of my mommy. All of the special
features about you, from your head down to your toes, as well as
all of your unique qualities from the inside out, came from God.

PRAY ABOUT IT

Dear Father, thank You for creating us! We are so grateful for
all of the special and unique traits You gave us. May we use our
bodies, minds, and talents for Your glory. Amen.

God Is Creating a Place for Us

"After I go and make a place for you, I will come back and take you with Me. Then you may be where I am."

John 14:3

Talk about it

What place do you think God is creating for us?

Read about it

God has not only created this home for us on earth, He is also creating a place for us in heaven. When we go to live with Him for eternity, that place where we will be has been specially designed for us. I don't know exactly what it will look like, but I'm certain that if God had it in mind for you and me it will be heavenly!

Pray about it

Dear God, we love how we get to benefit from everything Your hands have made. May our time spent here on earth be filled with opportunities to bless others. Amen.

God Is Good

How great is Your loving-kindness! You have stored it up for those who fear You. You show it to those who trust in You in front of the sons of men.

PSALM 31:19

TALK ABOUT IT

What have you learned about God that makes Him so good?

READ ABOUT IT

God goes before us and He is behind us. He created us. God is beautiful and holy. There are so many things we have been learning together about God through these devotions. God provides for us, restores us, and gives us rest. He has given us gifts, family, and strength in our weakness. God knows everything about us including the number of hairs on our head. He is powerful but also merciful, kind, compassionate, and loving toward us.

PRAY ABOUT IT

Dear God, we have so much evidence that helps us to say that You are truly good! Amen.

Jesus Was Once Little Too

The Child grew and became strong in spirit.
He was filled with wisdom and the
loving-favor of God was on Him.

LUKE 2:40

TALK ABOUT IT

What do you think it was like for Jesus when He was a little boy?

READ ABOUT IT

Jesus was little once too. The Bible says he grew up and was filled with wisdom. He was God's Son, who was watched over with great care by His heavenly Father. The Bible also says that as Jesus grew up He learned carpenter work from His earthly father, Joseph. God used everything that Jesus learned, in the temple and at home, for ministry. Everything you are learning right now—in school, church, home, and outside of the home—God will use and continue to do so for His good works.

PRAY ABOUT IT

Dear God, thank You for our childhood. We believe that everything we learn and do will be used by You for good. Amen.

God Gives Us Gifts

We all have different gifts that God has given to us by His loving-favor. We are to use them. If someone has the gift of preaching the Good News, he should preach. He should use the faith God has given him.

Romans 12:6

TALK ABOUT IT

What talents do you have that have been a blessing to others?

READ ABOUT IT

I just love watching you use the gifts that are inside of you, to be a gift to those around you! Did you know that God gave them to you? Like when you get good things at Christmastime or your birthday, God has placed these specially made abilities and talents within you. They are what make you unique! They are meant to be a blessing for those in our lives.

PRAY ABOUT IT

Dear God, please show us how to use the different gifts You have given us. May our unique qualities help us to share Your love with others. Amen.

Jesus Taught

The religious gathering was half over when Jesus
went to the house of God and taught.

JOHN 7:14

TALK ABOUT IT

What do you think Jesus taught about?

READ ABOUT IT

Jesus loved God. Because He loved God so much, He obeyed Him. Jesus knew how to obey God because He knew, read, and studied God's Word. The part of the Bible that Jesus taught is called the Old Testament. It's filled with story after story of God's faithfulness in the lives of those who were called by God. These stories are incredible accounts of God's love and deliverance on His people. We too can continue to read God's Word. As we do we'll grow to appreciate how Jesus taught.

PRAY ABOUT IT

Dear God, help us to continue to remain in You. Fill our hearts and minds with an overwhelming sense of Your presence and the desire to read Your Word. Amen.

Jesus Cried

Then Jesus cried.

JOHN 11:35

TALK ABOUT IT

Jesus knows what it's like to feel upset. Now that we know this, how does this make you feel?

READ ABOUT IT

As your mommy, it gives me great comfort to know that Jesus came to earth to be just like us. He walked through a lot of the same feelings and emotions we have experienced. He was hurt, treated poorly, and so much more. There are some things He endured that we may never fully experience or understand. It gives me great hope in knowing that Jesus walked through all of these things. This means He understands when you and I feel down or upset.

PRAY ABOUT IT

Dear Jesus, when we cry or feel upset, frustrated, or angry, You understand. You are our great Comforter. Thank You for knowing what it was like to walk in our shoes. Amen.

God Gives Us Leaders

Remember your leaders who first spoke God's Word to you. Think of how they lived, and trust God as they did.

HEBREWS 13:7

Talk about it

Who do you look up to? Or, who do you believe is a good example of how to behave?

Read about it

Whether it's our church pastor, a Sunday school volunteer, a teacher at school, or even an instructor, you have many people in your life who can be considered leaders. These are people who try to encourage you, guide you, give you advice, and set an example for how to act. I'm so grateful for all of these people in your life, because they have a lot of experience to share with you! Let's take some time to pray for them.

Pray about it

Dear God, thank You for putting people in our lives who help lead, guide, and direct us. We pray that they will experience Your love for them today! Amen.

God Is Invisible

We give honor and thanks to the King Who lives forever. He is the One Who never dies and Who is never seen. He is the One Who knows all things. He is the only God. Let it be so.

1 TIMOTHY 1:17

TALK ABOUT IT

If there is so much that God created, then why do you think He is never seen?

READ ABOUT IT

God created everything that we see, touch, hear, and taste. If God created all of these things, then why don't we see Him? We don't see God because He is in heaven looking down on us, taking care of the whole entire universe! Just because we don't see Him doesn't mean He isn't here. He is! The Bible says that it takes faith to believe in the things we do not see.

PRAY ABOUT IT

Dear God, when we lose heart and forget that You are right here with us, give us faith to believe. Amen.

God Is Spirit

"God is Spirit. Those who worship Him must worship Him in spirit and in truth."

JOHN 4:24

TALK ABOUT IT

What do you think it means to worship God in spirit and in truth?

READ ABOUT IT

To have God's Spirit within us means that the very basis of who He is dwells within us. God's spirit is good and benefits us all. It gives you and me the ability to do what would be impossible with our own strength alone. It also helps us worship God through our words, voice, and actions.

PRAY ABOUT IT

Dear God, we give thanks for Your Spirit that dwells in and among us. Teach us how to live with Your Spirit and truth. Amen.

God Gives Us Angels

For He will tell His angels to care for you
and keep you in all your ways.

PSALM 91:11

Talk about it

What do you think an angel looks and acts like?

Read about it

An angel can be described as a messenger, someone who performs a mission from God, or even resembling beauty or kindness. Sometimes we see pictures of them in human form wearing wings, a white robe, and even a halo over their head. Probably the most important characteristic of angels is they care for us. Even though we may never see an angel on this side of heaven, you and I can let God's love shine through us in such a way that we act just like an angel!

Pray about it

Dear God, thank You for giving us people who care for and watch over us. Through their actions, they are like an angel! We also thank You for spiritual angels. We know they spoke to and cared for Bible characters. Amen.

God Is Joy

Our hope comes from God. May He fill you with joy and peace because of your trust in Him. May your hope grow stronger by the power of the Holy Spirit.

ROMANS 15:13

TALK ABOUT IT

What gives you great joy?

READ ABOUT IT

There are a lot of things that can give us joy. It can be a hobby we're passionate about, a tradition we celebrate, or something simple like the smell of our favorite foods. While these things are all good, the joy we get from loving God is even better! Why? Because when we put our hope in Him, He gives us joy and peace. There are so many more wonderful things that come from the joy we receive from God. We don't have to do anything to get this joy.

PRAY ABOUT IT

Dear heavenly Daddy, thank You that we don't have to spend allowance money or accomplish something in order to get the joy that comes from You! Amen.

God Lives in You and Me

*Do you not know that you are a house of God
and that the Holy Spirit lives in you?*

1 CORINTHIANS 3:16

TALK ABOUT IT

In reading these devotionals, what have you learned so far about
how God lives inside of us?

READ ABOUT IT

The Bible uses the example of a house to help us better understand another way that God lives inside of us. Our body is like
a house. Inside our body lives the Holy Spirit. If we do not take
good care of our body, then we also aren't taking good care of
this dwelling place that the Holy Spirit lives in. Like a house, it's
important to clean it, treat it well, respect it, and so on. In the
same way God calls us to be responsible people with our body.

PRAY ABOUT IT

Dear God, thank You for living inside of us. Help us to treat our
body well, the way that You desire for it to be handled. Amen.

God Always Keeps His Promises

If we have no faith, He will still be faithful
for He cannot go against what He is.

2 TIMOTHY 2:13

TALK ABOUT IT

What are some promises that you have seen God keep in your life?

READ ABOUT IT

Promises are great but they are also hard to keep because we aren't perfect at following through on them. Yet, when someone does do what they say they intended to do we are often shocked. God, on the other hand, has tons of promises. They are all found in the Bible. And you know what? He keeps them all!

PRAY ABOUT IT

Dear God, You promise to be with us. Help us to remember that You keep all of Your promises. Amen.

God Wants Us to Ask

"Ask, and what you are asking for will be given to you. Look, and what you are looking for you will find. Knock, and the door you are knocking on will be opened to you."

MATTHEW 7:7

TALK ABOUT IT

What do you want to ask God for?

READ ABOUT IT

Just like you and I knock on a door when we want to enter into a room or a house, our prayers are a way of knocking on God's door. When we enter, then we get to go into God's presence and ask Him for what we need, through prayer. God might not always answer our prayers by giving us what we want. But He will certainly answer them with what we need.

PRAY ABOUT IT

Dear God, thank You for hearing our prayers and letting us ask. Amen.

You Are a Follower

"If you love each other, all men will know you are My followers."

JOHN 13:35

TALK ABOUT IT

What do you think it means to be a follower of Jesus?

READ ABOUT IT

There are many different ways that you and I can show each other and the people around us that we are followers of Jesus. A lot of the time, it's through our actions. How we love each other—sharing, caring, giving of our time and talents. I love seeing you show others that you follow Jesus. What is really cool is when you and I get to talk about Jesus to others. Sometimes that happens naturally when we tell people about the church we attend or how we are involved in different faith-filled activities.

PRAY ABOUT IT

Dear Jesus, help us to be more like You. May our actions and words show others that we truly follow You. Amen.

You Can Walk with God

Yes, even if I walk through the valley of the shadow of death, I will not be afraid of anything, because You are with me. You have a walking stick with which to guide and one with which to help. These comfort me.

PSALM 23:4

TALK ABOUT IT

The last time you went outside for a walk, what was it like?

READ ABOUT IT

I enjoy going for walks with family members like you! This is because I get to spend time with you. When we go for a walk outside or even inside like at a gym, we can pretend we're doing it with God. This is fun and helpful if we feel alone. God says He's always with us, and we always have Him by our side!

PRAY ABOUT IT

Dear God, let's go for a walk today. We want to hear about Your day and we want to tell You all about ours. Amen.

God Wants Us to Shine

Let your light shine in front of men. Then they will see the good things you do and will honor your Father Who is in heaven.

MATTHEW 5:16

TALK ABOUT IT

What do you think it means to let others see the good things you do?

READ ABOUT IT

When your room is completely dark at night, even the littlest light is noticeable. The same is true in our lives. When we do the right thing, say the right thing, and use our talents and abilities to bless others, we are letting the light that is within us shine outward. When this happens, people take notice. People can tell when we are living our lives with God's purpose, on purpose. Let's think of some ways we can let our lives radiate for Jesus!

PRAY ABOUT IT

Dear God, show us how to honor You in all that we say and do. Amen.

There Is Only One True God

Jesus said, "I am the Way and the Truth and the Life. No one can go to the Father except by Me."

John 14:6

Talk about it

What did Jesus mean when He said that He is the Way, the Truth, and the Life?

Read about it

Jesus is our Savior. He died on the cross to save us from our sins. There's nothing we can do to save ourselves from the wrong or bad things we do. The only thing we can do is put our faith, hope, and trust in Jesus. When we do, we can enter into a relationship with Him. By asking for our forgiveness, we are made right with God. Which means that someday we will get to live with Him forever! There is no other God like ours that promises these things for us.

Pray about it

Dear God, we are so grateful that You are the one true God. Amen.

God Is Holding You

"Do not fear, for I am with you. Do not be afraid, for I am your God. I will give you strength, and for sure I will help you. Yes, I will hold you up with My right hand that is right and good."

ISAIAH 41:10

TALK ABOUT IT

Even though you can't see Him, what are some examples that have shown you God is holding you?

READ ABOUT IT

God promises to always be with us. We might be filled with worry and fear, but guess what? He's always right beside us. The Bible says He holds us up with His right hand. He is our strength when we feel weak. As a mom, there have been numerous times I have felt weak physically or even emotionally. But when I pray to Him, I'm reminded that He holds me close like how you hold your stuffed animal.

PRAY ABOUT IT

Dear heavenly Daddy, thank You for never letting go of us! Amen.

God Is like the Sun

He is as bright as the sun. He has light shining
from His hand, where His power is hidden.

HABAKKUK 3:4

TALK ABOUT IT

What reminds you of the sun? Is there anything that is as bright,
or brighter, than the sun?

READ ABOUT IT

There are many things that might remind you of the sun like
lights that are very bright or objects that have a circular shape.
God is compared to being like the sun. He is bright and has
light that shines from His hand. We, His children, can reflect
this onto others.

PRAY ABOUT IT

Dear God, You are so bright and glorious! We want to shine for You
so that others can get a glimpse of Your love and beauty. Amen.

God Knows how You Feel

The Lord has loving-pity on those who fear Him,
as a father has loving-pity on his children.

PSALM 103:13

TALK ABOUT IT

What are some ways that you have shared your feelings with God?

READ ABOUT IT

Did you know that even before you speak, God knows how you feel? He still wants to hear from you though. He loves you so much that He has a lot of compassion for His children—and that includes you and me! It's not always easy to express our emotions to God, but when we call upon Him in prayer He promises to be there for us, to listen to us, and to help us. Isn't God good!

PRAY ABOUT IT

Dear heavenly Daddy, You are so good to us. We're just so grateful that You know how we feel. Thank You for being able to relate to us so well. Amen.

We All Make Mistakes

*For all men have sinned and have missed
the shining-greatness of God.*

ROMANS 3:23

TALK ABOUT IT

What's one thing you have done that you knew wasn't what God wanted you to do?

READ ABOUT IT

The word *sin* doesn't have a good sound to it. When we hear that word we might be reminded of the not-so-good things we've done. But you know what? I've come to appreciate this word. Why? Because it's a reminder that I need Jesus every day. As your mommy, it reminds me that I'm not perfect—I make mistakes and that's okay! I remember that Jesus is the one I need for help and guidance when I'm tempted to make a bad choice. I'm so thankful for God's forgiveness and letting us have do-overs.

PRAY ABOUT IT

Dear God, thank You for loving all of us even when we have made mistakes. Thank You for understanding us from the inside and out. Amen.

Jesus Died for Us

But God showed His love to us.
While we were still sinners, Christ died for us.

ROMANS 5:8

TALK ABOUT IT

What do you know about Jesus' death?

READ ABOUT IT

To hear that someone died for us doesn't sound good or pleasant. It sounds awful and sad. But there is good news in the fact that Jesus died for all of us. Jesus was born into this world. He was God's only Son who came down from heaven. He lived a sinless life and was nailed to a cross so that you and I could be made right with God. Without Jesus' willingness to do this for us and our ability to accept Him into our lives, we wouldn't get to experience true love, joy, peace, forgiveness, and life with Him in heaven!

PRAY ABOUT IT

Dear Jesus, we don't totally understand the beauty behind You leaving this earth. We are thankful for what You did for us, though. Help us to appreciate it. Amen.

God Wants Us to Move Mountains

Jesus said to them, "For sure, I tell you this: If you have faith and do not doubt, you will not only be able to do what was done to the fig tree. You will also be able to say to this mountain, 'Move from here and be thrown into the sea,' and it will be done."

MATTHEW 21:21

Talk about it

If you had help from someone, what do you think would be the biggest thing that you could move?

Read about it

When we move something that is really big and heavy, we use all of our strength to do it. There are things in life that we can't move physically without some help, though. When we ask God to join us in a challenging task, He can give us the faith, strength, help, and brainpower to do it.

Pray about it

Dear Jesus, when we do something that seems too much to handle, help us to trust that You will help us. Amen.

God Is the Creator of All Things

*"Our Lord and our God, it is right for You to have the
shining-greatness and the honor and the power.
You made all things. They were made and have
life because You wanted it that way."*

REVELATION 4:11

TALK ABOUT IT

What have you learned so far about God being our Creator?

READ ABOUT IT

Throughout these devotionals, we've learned that God is the Creator of everything! He created this earth and all of the things on it. He created you and me. He made people able to create all of the items we get to use and experience throughout our day. God is so amazing, awesome, and creative! Imagine what life would be like if all that we have wasn't created by God. There wouldn't be a lot for us to point to, to remember that He is good to us.

PRAY ABOUT IT

Dear Creator, thank You for creating *everything*! We are so blessed to put our faith, hope, and trust in You! Amen.

God's Word Is Truth for Us to Live By

"Make them holy for Yourself by the truth. Your Word is truth."

JOHN 17:17

TALK ABOUT IT

What have you learned so far about God's Word through these devotionals, at Sunday school, or at other church events?

READ ABOUT IT

Because you and I believe in Jesus we are called Christians. As a follower of Jesus, we believe that God's Word, which is scripture found in the Bible, is truth. As you and I grow and continue in our friendship with Jesus, we will come to find that many life experiences help us to know that God's Word is really true. There will be a lot of things in this world that will try to tell us His Word is false. But that is incorrect. It is good to live by what He says.

PRAY ABOUT IT

Dear God, help us to continue to remain in relationship with You. As we do, prove to us over and over again that Your words are true. Amen.

God Can Do Impossible Things

Jesus looked at them and said, "This cannot be done by men. But with God all things can be done."

MATTHEW 19:26

TALK ABOUT IT

What are some examples of things in your life that seemed like impossible tasks, but with God's help you were able to do it?

READ ABOUT IT

We all have areas in our life that look and feel impossible. Maybe it's your least favorite subject in school. Maybe it's the sport or activity that you don't feel good at. Maybe there's a classmate you thought was your friend but he or she has mistreated you. All of these situations can be considered impossible. But with God any situation can get better and turn into a miracle.

PRAY ABOUT IT

Dear Jesus, there are a lot of impossible-seeming things in our lives. We ask that Your Holy Spirit would fill us and enable us to do that which we think we can't do. Amen.

God Is Always in Charge

But the Lord is the true God. He is the living God and the King Who lives forever. The earth shakes at His anger. And the nations cannot last when He is angry.

JEREMIAH 10:10

TALK ABOUT IT

What has happened in your life that shows you God is always in charge?

READ ABOUT IT

When you are at home with me, you and I might think that I'm in charge. Yes, I want you to listen to me and I'm grateful when you do so with respect. But guess what? I'm really not the one in charge. And when Daddy is home, he isn't either. You know who is? God! That's right! God is in charge of everything, including our household. He lives and reigns over all that He created!

PRAY ABOUT IT

Dear God, sometimes we might be tempted to think we're the ones in charge of everything. But in reality, You are in charge! We're so grateful for that! Amen.

God Knows Every Detail

Even before I speak a word, O Lord,
You know it all.

PSALM 139:4

TALK ABOUT IT

What are some arts and crafts projects, or science projects, that you've worked on that have required *a lot* of detail?

READ ABOUT IT

There are so many projects that require a lot of time, focus, and energy. Whether it's a school art project, a science experiment, or a book report, there's a lot involved in getting things right. Even for me when I work on a project in the home like cooking, cleaning, or other work-related assignments, it is a lot of responsibility. When I have those moments where I feel overwhelmed by all there is to do, I turn to Jesus. He knows every single detail better than I do. He knows which step I need to take.

PRAY ABOUT IT

Dear God, You are the divine detail organizer! Show us which steps to take in all that we say and do. Amen.

God Is an Author

The Word (Christ) was in the beginning.
The Word was with God. The Word was God.

JOHN 1:1

TALK ABOUT IT

What stories about God do you like reading or hearing about?

PRAY ABOUT IT

Another way to describe God as the Creator over all is that He's also an Author. The words we read in the Bible were written by God. Our lives are also filled with stories. Countless stories, known as testimonies, that share with others about His goodness and faithfulness in our lives. I love hearing you share with me and others about what you've seen God do in your life. I get so much joy in telling others about God's ability to orchestrate everything together for good.

READ ABOUT IT

Dear Jesus, we love reading Your words in the Bible! We love hearing other people share their stories about You. Amen.

God Wants Us to Soar

But they who wait upon the Lord will get new strength. They will rise up with wings like eagles. They will run and not get tired. They will walk and not become weak.

ISAIAH 40:31

TALK ABOUT IT

If you were an eagle for a day, what do you think that would be like?

READ ABOUT IT

Eagles are amazing birds! They are beautiful to watch as they soar in the sky. Their wings are long and delicate. Did you know that we can be like an eagle too? God's Word says that when we wait on God, our faith will be renewed; we will go from feeling weak to being strong. As that strength rises up in us, we will be like an eagle. Let's soar together!

PRAY ABOUT IT

Dear heavenly Daddy, we just love the idea that we too can be like an eagle! Help us to soar in all that we do. Give us faith where it is lacking. Amen.

God Has Prepared Good Works for Us

We are His work. He has made us to belong
to Christ Jesus so we can work for Him.
He planned that we should do this.

EPHESIANS 2:10

TALK ABOUT IT

What are some tasks that you believe God has prepared for you to do?

READ ABOUT IT

God not only created us and knew us before we were even born, but He knows every detail about us. So much so that God planned way in advance good works for you and me to do. In this passage of scripture, we are referred to as a masterpiece—a work of art! We are His workmanship. He molded us together to be in relationship with Jesus. This is so that we can work for and represent Jesus in all that we say and do.

PRAY ABOUT IT

Dear God, how exciting that we get to work for You! Show us the tasks You want us to do so that we can make Your name great! Amen.

God Sent Us a Savior

We have seen and are able to say that the Father sent His Son to save the world from the punishment of sin.

1 JOHN 4:14

TALK ABOUT IT

What does it mean to you that Jesus is your Savior?

READ ABOUT IT

God sent Jesus down from heaven to earth. God used Mary to birth Jesus into this world. Jesus grew up and learned about the Word of God. He studied it and taught it. He also learned carpenter work from His father, Joseph. Jesus was baptized and did a lot of ministry during His short time here in the world. Then Jesus fulfilled what the prophets said He would do years before. He died on a cross for you and me. This allowed for Him to be the final sacrifice that saved the world from the punishment of sin.

PRAY ABOUT IT

Dear God, we are unable to save ourselves. Thank You for taking care of us! Amen.

God Wants Us to Plant Seeds

Isaac planted seeds in that land. And he gathered in the same year a hundred times as much as he had planted. The Lord brought good to him.

GENESIS 26:12

TALK ABOUT IT

Which flowers do you like the best? What vegetables do you like to eat?

READ ABOUT IT

A lot of flowers are extremely colorful. Many vegetables are delightfully delicious. Each one started out as a seed that was planted in dirt, nourished with water and other vitamins, before blossoming into the things we get to enjoy. Like planting flower or vegetable seeds, God wants us to plant seeds of faith and then help them grow with love and kindness. As we do, our lives will blossom!

PRAY ABOUT IT

Dear God, we want our lives to burst open with Your love! Show us how to plant seeds of faith so that others will get a taste of Your sweetness. Amen.

God Has a Mission for You

He said to them, "You are to go to all the world and preach the Good News to every person."

MARK 16:15

TALK ABOUT IT

What do you believe is your mission in life?

READ ABOUT IT

God has given you and me a calling. It can take many years for us to prayerfully figure out what that is. But throughout our life, as we remain in friendship with Jesus, we will always have a purpose. Our mission is to tell others about Jesus. No matter what we do, God can help us find creative ways to incorporate Him into our tasks. All we need to do is ask!

PRAY ABOUT IT

Dear God, whether we're at home, at school, in the car, or on the bus, and whether we're doing chores, playing with friends, meeting with neighbors, or doing other things, help us to stay on mission for You! Amen.

God Is Right beside Us

"No man will be able to stand against you all the days of your life. I will be with you just as I have been with Moses. I will be faithful to you and will not leave you alone."

JOSHUA 1:5

TALK ABOUT IT

In what ways do you know that God is right beside us?

READ ABOUT IT

We've been talking about the fact that God is all around us. If He is everywhere, that means He will never leave our side. Let's pretend that as we read this devotional together, God is sitting right beside us. I wonder what He would look like. I wonder what we would say to Him, or what He would say to us. While it is fun to imagine these things, the best part is that we don't have to. He already is here—and everywhere!

PRAY ABOUT IT

Dear Father, thank You for being so faithful to us even when we forget about You! Amen.

God Is Our Superhero

"O Lord God! See, You have made the heavens and the earth by Your great power and by Your long arm! Nothing is too hard for You!"

<small>JEREMIAH 32:17</small>

Talk about it

What important qualities do you think a superhero needs to have?

Read about it

Your favorite superhero can probably do some really cool things like flying over tall buildings, jumping really high, or running really fast! God has some very cool qualities too. Unlike the superheroes we read about in books or watch in the movies though, God is real! He's so real that the Bible says He created you and me! God is so powerful that He created the heavens and the earth too!

Pray about it

Dear God, thank You for being our Creator, Friend, and a real Superhero that we can count on. We're so grateful that nothing is too hard for You! Amen.

Jesus Is Alive

*"They did not find His body. They came back
saying they had seen angels in a special
dream who said that He was alive."*

LUKE 24:23

TALK ABOUT IT

If we can't see or touch Jesus, how do we know He is truly alive?

READ ABOUT IT

Jesus is alive! Where? Not under a rock or in a tomb. He's alive in this world, and in our hearts and minds. If we believe in Jesus, and we live a life that shows others His love, grace, and mercy, then that is one way Jesus lives on. Another way that Jesus is alive is in what we see around us. When we go outside to play, we get to see His creation at work, making all things new!

PRAY ABOUT IT

Dear Jesus, we believe that You are alive in us and in this world. Help us to carry on Your legacy. Amen.

Jesus Taught Us How to Pray

"Pray like this: 'Our Father in heaven,
Your name is holy.'"

MATTHEW 6:9

TALK ABOUT IT

What prayer is the scripture passage referring to?

READ ABOUT IT

There are a lot of prayers we can pray. Jesus taught us the "Our Father" prayer. We can also pray to God with our own words. Whether we are talking to Him out loud or silently, there are so many wonderful ways we can interact with Jesus on a regular basis. I love hearing you pray for family members, friends, our neighbors, and other people who mean a lot to you.

PRAY ABOUT IT

"Our Father in heaven, Your name is holy. May Your holy nation come. What You want done, may it be done on earth as it is in heaven. Give us the bread that we need today. Forgive us our sins as we forgive those who sin against us. Do not let us be tempted, but keep us from sin." (Matthew 6:9–13)

Jesus Is Compassionate

*When He got out of the boat, He saw many
people. He had loving-pity for them
and healed those who were sick.*

MATTHEW 14:14

TALK ABOUT IT

What do you think it means to be compassionate?

READ ABOUT IT

When you and I are compassionate, we have a feeling of deep
sympathy and sorrow for another person who is going through
a hard time. We also will feel like we wish we could help them in
some way or somehow take away their pain. It's not easy when
we walk through life with challenges. But you know what? We
can pray for that person. We can help them by asking if there's
anything they need.

PRAY ABOUT IT

Dear Jesus, help us to have the eyes to see and a heart that is full
of compassion toward others. We know that we can't fix every
situation, and so we trust that You are present. Amen.

Jesus Wants Us to Believe

Jesus said to him, "Why do you ask Me that?
The one who has faith can do all things."
MARK 9:23

TALK ABOUT IT

What do you have a hard time believing will come true?

READ ABOUT IT

Believing in ourselves or in others isn't exactly what Jesus was getting at. He wants us to not put our faith in ourselves: our talents, abilities, or the friends we have. Jesus wants us to believe in Him! When you and I focus on our Creator, the One who gave us this faith, there is a lot we can do! Let's ask Him to help us have the faith to believe again.

PRAY ABOUT IT

Dear Jesus, forgive us for the times we try to do things on our own. You created us and we need Your help in all that we do. May we desire to depend on You! Amen.

Jesus Loves Everyone

"A Son will be born to her. You will give Him the name Jesus because He will save His people from the punishment of their sins."

MATTHEW 1:21

TALK ABOUT IT

What are some ways that you share the love of Jesus with others?

READ ABOUT IT

Jesus came into this world for many reasons. One of them was to teach us what it truly means to love. Jesus said, "You must love the Lord your God with all your heart and with all your soul and with all your mind and with all your strength.' This is the first Law. The second Law is this: 'You must love your neighbor as yourself.' No other Law is greater than these" (Mark 12:30–31). Jesus reminds us to love as He does.

PRAY ABOUT IT

Dear God, we confess that we aren't good at loving all people. Sometimes it's really hard to show love toward those closest to us too. Please give us the ability to do so. Amen.

Jesus Wants to Save Everyone

What I say is true and all the world should receive it. Christ Jesus came into the world to save sinners from their sin and I am the worst sinner.

1 TIMOTHY 1:15

TALK ABOUT IT

Why do you think it can be so hard for someone to accept Jesus into their life?

READ ABOUT IT

Not everyone likes the fact that they can't fix themselves, or even save themselves. So to accept the fact that someone else did it for them can be hard. To accept that a person *willingly* did it for them can seem unbelievable. Why would someone want to save sinners? Love. We don't always feel like we want to love, though. Which is why receiving Jesus into our hearts is a choice. Is it one that you want to make?

PRAY ABOUT IT

Dear Jesus, we confess that we sin. We want to make things right with You. Forgive us and help us start a great friendship with You! Amen.

We Are like Sheep

"Then you would go to your house and call your friends and neighbors. You would say to them, 'Be happy with me because I have found my sheep that was lost.'"

Luke 15:6

Talk about it

Why do you think we are God's sheep?

Read about it

In the Bible, we read about the picture-story of the lost sheep. Jesus uses this to illustrate just how much He loves us, even when we walk away from Him. When we do something wrong, often called sin, it creates distance between us and God. But God loves you and me so much that He is like a shepherd that will not allow distance to come between us. He is glad to come to us and carry us back to Him, especially when we realize our mistakes and ask for forgiveness.

Pray about it

Dear God, thank You for loving us and accepting us no matter what we say or do that hurts You. Amen.

Jesus Loves Children

But Jesus said, "Let the little children come to Me.
Do not stop them. The holy nation of heaven
is made up of ones like these."
Matthew 19:14

Talk about it

What has it been like for you to read these devotions with me?

Read about it

When you and I have this special time together, we are growing in our relationship with each other. I love that! When we have this time together, we are also growing in our faith and in our relationship with Jesus. He loves that! Jesus loves little children like you, and big kids like me! So let us continue to enjoy these devotions together knowing that He welcomes us anytime, just the way we are.

Pray about it

Dear God, we are so blessed to be Your children. Thank You that nothing can stop us from spending time with You! Amen.

Jesus Is the Son of God

A voice came from heaven and said, "You are My much-loved Son. I am very happy with You."

MARK 1:11

TALK ABOUT IT

When you hear that Jesus is God's much-loved Son, what does that mean to you?

READ ABOUT IT

Just like you are my child, Jesus is God's Son. When Jesus lived on earth, it was declared from above, where God lives, that Jesus was His Son. As a result, Jesus is your Savior and He cares for you with an unconditional love! You are also His beloved child. So cared for that Jesus came down from heaven to earth, and died so that our sins could be forgiven and so that we can have eternal life with Him.

PRAY ABOUT IT

Dear Jesus, we love You! We are so grateful to be united with You in Your family here on earth and in heaven. Amen.

Jesus Is Coming Back

The Lord God says, "I am the First and the Last, the beginning and the end of all things. I am the All-powerful One Who was and Who is and Who is to come."

REVELATION 1:8

TALK ABOUT IT

What do you think it was like when people realized Jesus was the king they had been waiting for?

READ ABOUT IT

When people realized that Jesus was the long-awaited king, the Bible says that many didn't even know it. They had their own ideas of what they thought the Messiah would look like or be like. Some realized He was the one they had waited for when He did miracles or taught. Jesus is going to come back to earth again someday. I pray that when He does, many people will accept Him.

PRAY ABOUT IT

Dear Jesus, thank You for coming once and thank You for the promise that You are coming a second time. Amen.